IT WAS A raucous time of duels with words and swords, the fifty-year period between the War of 1812 and the Civil War called the Age of Jackson. It was, in its own special way, a time of revolution. People weren't killing each other, and mobs didn't riot in the streets. But enormous changes were shaking and transforming America. And a generation of political geniuses appeared, to wrestle with the nation's prospects and with each other. The men? Andrew Jackson. Daniel Webster. Henry Clay. John C. Calhoun. Martin Van Buren. And the issues? How to make America truly democratic. How to hold the Union together, when slavery was threatening to tear it apart. What to do with the Indians, who seemed to many to stand in the way of America's westward "destiny." And—probably most important to us today—how to solve the fierce power struggle between the President and the Congress.

The revolutionary Age of Andrew Jackson changed much of America's way of life. It established the nation's basic political practices and patterns. It stands at the beginning of the modern America we have inherited.

THE
REVOLUTIONARY

AGE OF
ANDREW JACKSON

Robert V. Remini

HARPER & ROW,
PUBLISHERS
New York, Hagerstown,
San Francisco, London

(title page) The Verdict of the People, by George Caleb Bingham, shows how the American people, in ever-increasing numbers, were creating a democracy during the Jacksonian period. Here they express their will via the ballot box on election day in a little Missouri town. The clerk, left, reads the results from the courthouse steps.

THE REVOLUTIONARY AGE OF ANDREW JACKSON
Copyright © 1976 by Robert V. Remini

Library of Congress Catalog Card Number: 74-2623
Trade ISBN 0-06-024856-4
Harpercrest ISBN 0-06-024857-2

FIRST EDITION

For Joan

CONTENTS

BOOK III
THE GROWTH OF PRESIDENTIAL POWER

List of Illustrations

Acknowledgments

THIS BOOK IS based on extensive reading of manuscripts and other documents of the Age of Jackson, particularly private letters by the major figures, speeches in Congress, presidential papers and messages, and other official and unofficial sources. Many conversations reproduced here, especially those involving Jackson, are taken from James Parton, *The Life of Andrew Jackson* (New York, 1860). Others come from Martin Van Buren's *Autobiography* (Washington, 1920) and Thomas Hart Benton's memoir of his career in the Senate, *Thirty Years' View* (New York, 1865). The description of Jackson's inauguration is largely based on the letters of Margaret Bayard Smith, the wife of a Maryland Senator: *The First Forty Years of Washington Society Portrayed by the Family Letters of Mrs. Samuel Harrison Smith,* edited by Gaillard Hunt (New York, 1906).

Contemporary narratives by travelers and foreign visitors have been quoted extensively since many of them met the principal figures of the period and described their impressions. They also traveled around the country and talked with Americans from every social and economic class. Two Englishwomen, in particular, provide extraordinary insights into American life and character. Sometimes they are devastatingly critical. Harriet Martineau, who wrote *Society in America* (New York, 1837) and dined in the White House, rather liked Henry Clay but thought John C. Calhoun a "cast-iron man." Frances Trollope, who wrote *Domestic Manners of the Americans* (London, 1832), thought rather poorly of American manners.

Other colorful descriptions of American life in the 1830s from which I have quoted are: Michel Chevalier, *Society, Manners, and Politics in the United States* (Boston, 1839); Captain Frederick Marryat, *A Diary in America* (London, 1839); J.S. Buckingham, *America* (London, 1841); Thomas Hamilton, *Men and Manners in America* (Philadelphia, 1833); and Alexis de Tocqueville, *Democracy in America* (New York, 1835).

Now that I've duly acknowledged my obligations to Jackson, his friends and enemies, and other writers of the period for supplying many of the ideas and words that form the core of this book, I should like to express a more immediate and personal obligation to several people who share whatever merit this book contains. First, Sam B. Smith and Harriet C. Owsley, editor and associate editor of "The Papers of Andrew Jackson," a project located at the Hermitage in Tennessee to publish all the important documents relating to Jackson's life. Over the years they have provided me enormous personal and professional support as we strove together to uncover every last scrap of Jackson material, wherever it might be, both here and abroad. The Ladies' Hermitage Association, charged with the responsibility of maintaining the Hermitage mansion and grounds, has shown extraordinary wisdom and imagination in recognizing their charge not only to preserve the physical remains of Jackson's life but his place and importance in American history. Both directly and indirectly the Association has advanced Jacksonian scholarship in countless ways, the latest being its unstinting support of the publication of the Jackson papers.

I owe a special and deep debt of gratitude to Elaine Edelman, a truly great editor, who originally invited me to write this book and then prodded me to make it worthy of the people who crowd these pages. In this final version of the manuscript there are deep traces of her editorial skill and personal commitment, and I am proud to acknowledge her unique and valuable contributions.

Finally, my daughter Joan also wanted me to write this book, and for all kinds of good reasons it is now hers.

Robert V. Remini
April 1975
Wilmette, Illinois

THE REVOLUTIONARY
AGE OF
ANDREW JACKSON

BOOK I
A NEW AGE

(overleaf) The rapid pulse of commerce and business during the "go-ahead" years can be felt in this busy scene of lower Broadway when New York was becoming the nation's financial capital. People crowd streets and sidewalks, hustling to bring about a dynamic, industrial, modern America.

1

A Changing Society

THE NATION WAS in the midst of a profound revolution when Andrew Jackson entered the White House on March 4, 1829, as the seventh President of the United States. It was not a violent revolution. People weren't killing one another. No mobs rioted through the streets to vent their rage. Nevertheless, momentous changes were occurring throughout the country, changes that transformed American society and government. Indeed it is not an exaggeration to say that many of the characteristics commonly thought of today as being typically American developed during this "revolutionary" era.

Historians call it the Age of Jackson and think of it as the period in American history roughly bridging the years from the end of the War of 1812 to the coming of the Civil War. But whatever the title and however it is called, it was an age of change, an age of innovation, an age of reform.

The United States was only forty years old at the time of Jackson's election to the presidency. When the nation began in 1789 as a republic under the Constitution, it had a small population of a few million people occupying thirteen states strung along the Atlantic seaboard. Its society had been confined, huddled along the coastline for more than a hundred and fifty years, since colonization first began. The Appalachian Mountains served as a barrier to the west, but also provided protection against the terrors of the vast wilderness that stretched beyond. During the entire colonial period of American history, settlers had hardly moved more than a few hundred miles inland from the Atlantic shore. Most colonists were farmers and lived in small communities in which there was close contact. The ties of family, church, and community were strong and produced a sense of security and belonging. It was a closely knit society and relatively stable. Some even thought there was overcrowding!

With the conclusion of the American Revolution, a genuine westward movement began. Then, starting early in the nineteenth century, the country burst its narrow confines. Within a few decades the nation was converted from an insulated, agrarian society squeezed between ocean and mountains into a dynamic, industrial society sprawled across a three-thousand-mile continent. Gone were the old ties of family, church, and community; gone, too, was the security they provided. A people so long hemmed in by a mountain chain scrambled over it and raced across the fertile valleys on the other side, reaching the Mississippi and fording it, clearing the land and creating new states in the process. It had taken nearly two centuries for Americans to occupy a ribbon of land hardly more than a hundred miles in width. During the next sixty years, they would go the rest of the distance across the continent to the Pacific Ocean, nearly three thousand miles. A tiny rural nation struggling to maintain its existence became a continental power whose future greatness was now assured.

In the forty years from the adoption of the Constitution to the inauguration of President Jackson, the thirteen states had grown to twenty-four. In the South and Southwest, Alabama, Mississippi, Louisiana, Tennessee, Kentucky, and Missouri had been added to the Union. Farther north, Maine, Ohio, Indiana, and Illinois had achieved statehood. The admission of Missouri during the 1820s was particularly significant. Not only did it provoke an open controversy over slavery (which was resolved by the Missouri Compromise that retained a balance in the Union between free and slave states), but Missouri was the first state that lay totally west of the Mississippi River to enter the Union. It marked a great stride in westward expansion.

But geographical expansion was not the only change produced in this "revolutionary" age. There were social, psychological, economic, and political changes that influenced the history not only of the United States but of the entire western world.

American society itself had changed. It was different. Everyone could see that. "Our age is wholey [*sic*] of a different character from the past," said Senator Daniel Webster of Massachusetts. "Society is full of excitement." Foreign visitors instantly noticed this excitement when they talked with people. The spirit was contagious. It was a spirit of "Go ahead." "The whole continent presents a scene of *scrambling* and roars with greedy hurry," observed an Englishman. "Go ahead! is the order of the day."

More than that. "*Go ahead* is the real motto of the country," commented most foreigners who analyzed the mood of America during the Jacksonian age. But precisely what did that mean?—"Go ahead." For individuals it meant the consuming need to make money. There was a restless, driving desire to be better off, and this was the ambition of all classes of society, none excepted. "No man in America is contented to be poor, or expects to continue so," stated one magazine of the time. Americans believed that in Europe children were lucky if they could maintain the station and income of their parents. Lucky if they did not slide to a lower social and financial condition. Not so in America. In America it was expected that children would improve their station, make more money than their parents, get a higher-paying job, find a better life. That's what "go ahead" was all about.

So the sons took off. They vaulted over the mountains seeking to satisfy their ambitious yearning in the west. They wanted something better than a slice of a small inheritance, and they believed they could find it away from home. Some were hardly into their teenage years when they bid farewell to their families to search for that better life. There was only one way to describe them. Restless, searching, driving. By the time of Jackson's inauguration in 1828 it was the prevailing mood of the country.

For instance, way out "west," Chicago—a tiny settlement just getting started on the high prairie above the shore of Lake Michigan—crawled with people. And the buying and selling! the land speculation! the agitation and activity! It stunned every person who visited the town. The land speculation was especially amazing. The times and places of land sales were announced by a black man, dressed all in scarlet and carrying an enormous scarlet flag, sitting astride a snow-white horse: Lord, they said, he was beautiful to see. At every street corner where he stopped to sing out his announcement, a crowd of people flocked around him.

This land mania infected everyone. New arrivals to Chicago were propositioned constantly. As they walked down the streets, storekeepers hailed them from their doors. "Hey! You want to buy a farm?" they shouted.

One young lawyer in Chicago claimed he realized five hundred dollars a day by merely making out titles to land. Another said he realized within two years—two years, mind you—"*ten times* as much money as he had before fixed upon as a competence for life."

But there was a price—a high price—Americans paid for "go ahead." They no longer had the security of a tightly integrated society in which all persons had a place and knew their responsibilities and what was expected of them. In the past everybody had belonged; all were important to each other and to society as a whole. Individuals, no matter what they did for a living or what their social position, had the comforting knowledge that they were needed and wanted. And this strong sense of belonging and participation was buttressed by powerful links of family, of community responsibility, and of church membership. But "go ahead" changed all that. With men and women on the move, scrambling to achieve material success, they had no time for the needs of others. Their responsibility was to themselves and their own goals. Never mind the neighbors. Let neighbors keep their distance and mind their own business. The needs of the community in maintaining a stable society were problems for "others" to bother about—whoever those others might be. Besides, in what now became a constant moving from place to place, few people had a real attachment to any one community. Not like the old days, when families lived for generations in a particular town. Now one was almost expected to keep moving geographically if he hoped to "go ahead" financially. And with sons breaking free from the family at an early age to seek their futures and fortunes, and girls marrying in their teens and taking off with their ambitious husbands, the strong ties of family as an important component in American society were gravely weakened. Families dispersed so quickly that the sense of belonging that characterized colonial life vanished.

This left a terrible void. And to some extent the social history of Americans during the first half of the nineteenth century is the history of the search for something to fill that void. If they no longer had family or community or membership in a particular church to give them security, they needed something else to fill their lives and give them meaning and purpose. In time most of them found it in work—the hard, persistent application of their talents and strengths to achieve their ambitions. Americans had always believed in work. It was part of their Puritan past, but now it had an urgency that foreigners instantly detected the moment they set foot on this continent. It pulsed throughout society. One foreigner claimed that the first command of American society was to "Work!" And no excuses. "Work," he wrote, and "at eighteen you shall get . . . more than a captain in Europe. You shall live in plenty, be well clothed, well housed, and able to save." Everything else followed from this command. "Be attentive to your work, be sober and religious, and you will find a devoted and submissive wife; you will have a more comfortable home than many of the higher classes in Europe. . . . Work, and if the fortunes of business should be against you and you fail, you shall soon be able to rise again, for a failure is nothing but a wound in battle."

Thus the first article of the American faith was simply this: Keep your nose to the grindstone, lead a clean and sober life, and you cannot fail. And what was the reward? Money. Money and those creature comforts that make life more bearable. It also brought social standing, recognition that one was engaged in useful pursuits, a judgment from society that one's life was a "success."

Following this Puritan work ethic, a young man of the Age of Jackson began earning a living by the time he was fifteen. By twenty-one he was expected to be established, to have his own office or workshop or farm or whatever it was that constituted his "living." And by twenty-one a man was expected to be married. Indeed, if he was not established and not married by twenty-one, society judged him peculiar and no-account. "He who is an active and useful member of society," wrote one visitor, "who contributes his share to augment the national wealth and increase the numbers of the population, he only is looked upon with respect and favor."

Women's duties were rigidly fixed from the moment of their birth. They were expected to be wives and mothers. They were expected to be submissive—first to father, then husband—loving, gentle, and domestic. Interestingly, at the very moment the family condition was weakened, Americans exalted marriage and regarded the tie between husband and wife as the central moral bulwark of society. At the same

7

time women enjoyed precious few "rights," they were placed on a pedestal and revered for their "piety" and "purity"—in short, they were commissioned the moral guardians of the human race. It was in the Jacksonian era that the exaggerated, if not distorted, views of women as to their gentleness, frailty, piety, morality, and purity developed. During this period the pronounced male affection for his mother—"Momism"—is first observed. And the higher woman rose on her pedestal, the more she lost ground in attempting to gain equality with males.

But whether one was male or female, the habits and tone of American life as established in the early nineteenth century were those of an "exclusively working people." From the moment Americans got up in the morning they were hard at work and continued at it until bedtime. Rarely did they permit pleasure to distract them. Only public affairs or politics had the right to claim their time for a few minutes. And only on Sunday did Americans refrain from business, not only because of the strictures of organized religion but because it supposedly proved them God-fearing and therefore sober and clean-living. "The American of the North and Northwest," wrote one observer, "whose character now sets the tone in the United States is permanently a man of business."

According to Europeans, American men even looked as if they were built for work, as if work were God's intended objective "when He fashioned the American." Tall, slender, lithe, he had "no equal" in promptly responding to the demands of business, whatever those demands might be. This Yankee type had a hawkish look about him that bespoke shrewdness and cunning. Though gangling, rawboned, and sinewy, he was a clear-eyed, sharp-witted, practical man of affairs with educated instincts to search out the sources of wealth.

As Americans succeeded in improving their own individual economic lot, they necessarily advanced the well-being of the country. They fanned out across the continent, clearing land, planting, harvesting, searching all the avenues leading to personal prosperity. They galvanized the economy and raised the standard of living.

There was a noticeable jump in the standard of living during the first half of the nineteenth century. During the long colonial period the standard of living had remained relatively stable and relatively low. Then, with the building of a free, independent domestic economy, the standard of living for most white Americans rose sharply.

Building a free, independent economy was important in the

8

revolutionary changes that occurred in America during the Age of Jackson. But it took time. When the nation first won its independence its economy was based almost exclusively on international trade. But during the final years of the War of 1812 much of the nation's coastline was blockaded. Its ships could not get in or out of its harbors. Consequently the country had to look to its own resources and not rely on trade with Europe. It was forced to build its own internal economy. So capital investments went into industry and manufactures, instead of shipping. Manufactures, especially textile products, multiplied rapidly. Although industrial expansion was the most dramatic, agriculture—the main preoccupation of most Americans—also increased its productivity.

Thus, the War of 1812 compelled the United States to take a new direction into rapid industrial development. The factory system, which had already begun in Great Britain, was introduced when plans of a newly invented textile machine were secreted into the United States. And because of the great natural resources in the country, like coal, iron and water power, and because of the increasing labor supply provided through immigration, the Industrial Revolution quickly established itself in America.

What happened in Lowell, Massachusetts, is a good example. Lowell was a quiet, pleasant little New England town situated at the confluence of the Concord and Merrimack Rivers. Most of its inhabitants were farmers. But with the coming of the Industrial Revolution to Lowell in 1820, because of the easy access to water power, the town became a booming manufacturing center. By the late 1820s there were a variety of factories in Lowell: flour mills, glass works and machine manufacturers, iron and copper works, foundries and shoe factories. But the principal industry in the town was its textile mills. Once it was fully mechanized Lowell manufactured upwards of fifty-two million yards of cotton cloth a year. By the use of man-made canals the waterpower generated was sufficient to operate 286,000 spindles.

But the industrialization of America was not simply the product of hundreds of factories turning out useful manufactures. There was also a "Transportation Revolution." Again it was the War of 1812 that set the revolution in motion. For the war reminded Americans of the perpetual danger of invasion by British troops from Canada. The need to move troops rapidly to repel invasion produced a demand for improved transportation and soon the nation engaged in a gigantic program of building roads, bridges, highways, turnpikes and canals. Improved transportation and communication were first seen as essential to the nation's safety, but they also stimulated commerce and industry.

The individual states led the way in this feverish rush to construct public works. The Pennsylvania Turnpike stretched from Philadelphia to Lancaster and the Wilderness Road cut across Virginia into Kentucky. The great National Road, begun in 1811 from Cumberland, Maryland, steadily inched its way westward nine hundred miles to Vandalia, Illinois, in 1838. New York began the mighty Erie Canal in 1817; completed eight years later, it linked the Hudson River to Lake Erie in a 363-mile stretch that permitted water transportation from the Atlantic Ocean to the Great Lakes. This canal made Ohio, Michigan, Indiana, and Illinois accessible to the thousands of European immigrants who soon came flooding through the port of New York. The value of land and of personal property in New York City rose sixty percent in five years and the Canal itself earned nearly a million dollars annually. The activity generated by the Canal enormously enhanced the wealth, population, and power of New York. It became the Empire State. Its immediate and visible success prompted other states to imitate this colossal feat, and during the 1820s a mania of canal building swept the country. In Pennsylvania a canal system linked Philadelphia with Pittsburgh. Cleveland on Lake Erie was joined to Portsmouth on the Ohio River by canal. And the building of the Illinois and Michigan Canal in the late 1830s and 1840s made it possible to travel by water from Lake Michigan to the Illinois River and from there to the Mississippi River. When the War of 1812 had ended there had been less than a hundred miles of canals in the United States. Twenty-five years later there were well over three thousand miles.

Better and quicker transportation aided this generation of hustling Americans to drive faster and deeper into the continent. Moving goods, supplies, manufactured articles, and agricultural staples from one section of the country to another was important in developing a free, independent domestic economy.

Still, canals and roads and bridges and turnpikes paled in significance when compared to the railroads. The railroads, which began to be built late in the 1820s, were absolutely central to industrializing America. Not only did they quicken travel and westward expansion across the continent—burrowing through, around, and over mountains—but they created new communities and, with them, additional markets. Wherever the railroad stopped, or changed direction, or intersected with other forms of transportation, a town or city sprang up. Railroads became lifelines stringing communities of people together over thousands of miles, from the Atlantic coast to the Great Plains beyond the Mississippi River and eventually reaching the Pacific coast. They were the nation's arteries, providing a constant flow of people and commodities from city to town to remote rural community and pumping economic life to all the areas they served. Furthermore, the railroads attracted financial capital in the form of investments from foreigners as well as Americans who sensed the opportunity to make an economic killing. Investors found railroads irresistible. They were drawn by the prospect of enormous profits, particularly after the federal government lavished the roads with land grants and other subsidies to encourage their growth. Within a few decades a stupendous amount of money was generated, much of it squandered, much of it badly used, much of it siphoned off by swindlers. But enough remained to build a nation. It was the coming of the railroad to Chicago, for example, that catapulted that hustling lakeside community of land jobbers into a roaring metropolis of merchant princes, the hub city of the entire West.

The first railroad in the United States was built in Massachusetts in 1828. But the important history of railroading really began the next year with the construction of the Baltimore and Ohio Railroad. Symbolically, the man who lifted the first spadeful of dirt to start that construction was Charles Carroll of Carrollton, the last surviving signer of the Declaration of Independence. To some observers it seemed appropriate that a man who had signed the document that brought forth an independent nation should also, by the action of a shovel, signal the beginning of a modern, industrial society for that nation. Within two years the B & O consisted of thirteen miles of road; but within another six years over one thousand miles of track stretched across eleven states.

The speed and ease with which Americans accepted and adopted modern industrial tools won the admiration of foreign visitors. It explained how a society was revolutionized. The American, said one foreigner, was remarkable in his ability to adjust himself—and anything else for that matter—to the demands of business. "No one else can conform so easily to new situations and circumstances; he is always ready to adopt new processes and implements or to change his occupation. Where in Europe young men write poems or novels, in America,

The "Transportation Revolution" began symbolically with the opening of the Erie Canal in 1825. New York's Governor DeWitt Clinton poured a barrel of Lake Erie water into the Atlantic Ocean, in what was called the "marriage of waters." The Canal cut the cost of transporting a ton of goods from Buffalo to New York from $100 to $15.

especially Massachusetts and Connecticut, they invent machines and tools.'' The American "is a mechanic by nature." He prizes gadgets and tools which make life more agreeable.

It was extraordinary how many important tools and gadgets were invented during this Jacksonian age! Many raised the standard of living. Some changed society and the economy. Even so-called minor inventions altered social life. For example, the invention of a special bit permitted cutting ice so that large chunks could be shipped without melting and then brought into city homes. Having ice for refrigeration meant that people could congregate in cities where, unable to produce their own food, they could still enjoy fresh food almost anytime they wanted. This ability to store food was vital to the growth of American cities.

At this time, too, the process of canning foods was developed, an invention that had a most profound impact on the eating habits of the American family. "Opening a can" to prepare lunch or dinner became a way of life for some. Americans, by and large, are not gourmets and never were—we are a nation of hamburger and hot-dog eaters—so the can made it very easy to dispense with all the preparation needed for fixing meals. It left more time for work.

Americans proved how inventive and adaptable they were in other ways. For instance, when oil was discovered in Pennsylvania, there seemed to be no apparent use for it except as a base for "snake oil" in medicine shows. But some "go-ahead" Americans used their ingenuity to create a market for it by developing a special lamp—a kerosene lamp—to burn the oil, and then trumpeted it around the country as an inexpensive and efficient source of illumination for the home. With that, a new business—indeed several new businesses—were off and running. But what was so "typically American" about all this was the way the opportunity was handled. Here was a product of little apparent use and with no market. Americans created the market. They came up with a gadget to burn the oil and then successfully peddled it with a massive advertising campaign.

Also during this age there were some spectacular inventions: the mechanical reaper for harvesting grain, invented by Cyrus H. McCormick in 1831; Charles Goodyear's process of vulcanizing rubber in 1839; Samuel F.B. Morse's telegraph in 1844; Samuel Colt's revolver in 1835; and Elias Howe's sewing machine in 1846. These were only the most important. Anaesthesia, discovered by a dentist

13

named William T.G. Morton in 1842—the discovery was also claimed by at least three other men—was one of the most valuable and important discoveries in the entire history of medicine.

What made these inventions so spectacular was that they revolutionized entire industries, created new industries, or developed new processes which advanced the industrialization of the nation. The new companies resulting from these inventions attracted additional capital into the country. New jobs were created. New markets found. By 1840 the country—especially the North and Northwest—was hurrying toward rapid industrialization. The country had begun converting from a rural and agricultural society to an urban and industrial one. There was a long way yet to go, but it was the beginning.

In the South the push toward industrialization was not so obvious, although some industrialization could be found. But even in that section there was enormous economic energy. The principal business was cotton, and eventually—that is, just prior to the Civil War—the South was growing two-thirds of the total world supply of cotton. The plantation system widely utilized in the South was based on black slavery. However morally indefensible, the system—in the opinion of some recent historians—was far more efficient and economical than the methods of farming pursued in the Northwest.

But whether North or South, East or West, the nation during the Age of Jackson throbbed and pulsed with energy. "Life consists in motion," wrote one visitor, and in the relentless need to be better off—to make it. When foreigners chided Americans about their pursuit of wealth, they were promptly corrected. Americans hotly denied that they valued wealth more than other people. They simply insisted that the pursuit of money in other countries, especially in Europe, was necessarily confined to a very small group of people—the privileged few, the upper class, the aristocracy—while in America it was open to all. Everyone should have the right to make money if he had the drive and desire to go after it. That's what freedom was all about. "In this country," wrote one commentator, "there are no established limits within which the hopes of any class of society must be confined as in other countries." Here children are expected to do better than their parents because here there is "equality of opportunity," which in turn has produced "universal ambition and restless activity."

When Jacksonians talked about equality they were not thinking in literal terms of everyone being equal. They realized that everyone was not equal—and maybe there was some advantage to that. Talents varied, abilities differed. What they did believe and were committed to was the notion of equality of *opportunity*. Everyone should have the opportunity to make it, to get ahead, to achieve financial success. No one should have special privileges that work to the disadvantage of others. Thus, one of the functions of government was to see to it that the race for success was a fair contest. Government must serve as a referee among all classes in society and prevent any one from gaining an advantage over the others.

Privileges, or what Jacksonians called ''artificial distinctions,'' that blocked equality of opportunity had to be removed by governmental action. And Americans were particularly conscious of political and economic privileges. Political privileges included the right to vote or hold office because of wealth or social standing. Restricting the right to vote to persons owning at least one hundred dollars worth of property had been the classic form of political privilege during the colonial era. But this practice started to fade rapidly as Americans dissolved their political ties to Great Britain and geographical ties to the Atlantic shoreline. As they moved westward Americans established local governments that did away with property qualifications, giving every white man over the age of twenty-one the right to vote and hold office. Consequently, when Western states such as Ohio, Indiana, Illinois, and Missouri applied for admission into the Union, their constitutions specifically guaranteed white manhood suffrage. In no time the influence of the West was felt in the East. Several of the older states whose constitutions had been written in the eighteenth century called new constitutional conventions in the 1820s and not only liberalized the franchise but democratized the entire political process. For example, though several state constitutions had originally provided that presidential electors be chosen by the state legislatures, the constitutional conventions of the 1820s abolished this practice and provided *popular* election of presidential electors.*

Economic privilege, on the other hand, took the form of monopolies or exclusive rights and franchises which granted advantages to some but denied them to others. These privileges were particularly hated because,

---

*The electoral system written into the Constitution provides for what is in fact indirect election of the President. Each state is allotted a number of electors equal to its number of representatives and senators in Congress. These electors are appointed as the states direct. In the beginning they were chosen by state legislatures, later by popular vote. Yet as late as 1860 electors in South Carolina were still chosen by the legislature.

granted by the government, whether state or national, they institutionalized inequality. When the Massachusetts legislature, for example, gave a charter to the Charles River Bridge Company to build the one and only bridge across the Charles River to connect Boston with Cambridge, and to charge a fee to anyone using the bridge, the people in the area protested. They wanted a free bridge. When a second company was proposed to satisfy the public clamor, the Charles River Bridge Company pointed to the clause in its charter which implied *exclusive* rights to the bridge business over the Charles. Eventually the entire matter landed in the United States Supreme Court, where the right of a state to grant exclusive privileges at the expense of community need and desire was struck down. Monopolies were so despised in this age committed to equality of opportunity that one writer went so far as to define liberty "as nothing more than the total absence of all MONOPOLIES of all kinds, whether of rank, wealth or privilege."

To most Americans, therefore, the elimination of privilege necessarily provided equality of opportunity. They regarded privilege as synonymous with "aristocracy," a term held in the highest contempt since the Revolution. Conversely, "democracy" was defined as the removal of every political and economic barrier blocking the progress of all citizens in their quest for personal freedom and material happiness. If this nation was to be truly democratic, editorialized the New York *Evening Post*, then there must come the end "of all privilege." Indeed, the writer continued, every democratic advance achieved in this country in the past had come as a result of "breaking down the privileges of a few."

The job of the government was clearly understood as assisting this process. Not that Americans wanted a government that constantly intruded on their lives and private affairs. Far from it. As a matter of fact one Washington newspaper published a brief motto over its masthead: "The World Is Governed Too Much." And this conviction was shared by many Americans. Most people seemed to feel the proper function of government was in the role of referee or honest broker. The government should see to it that no one group or class in society gained advantages over others, particularly government-granted advantages. Thus, monopolies had to be abolished and voting rights equalized. In the contest for the pursuit of happiness, the government had to make certain that the contest was a fair one. No one must have a head start as the result of government-granted preference.

16

When all is said and done, two basic qualities tell the most about Americans in this Jacksonian era. First, they were materialists. They were out to make it. They wanted money, and they wanted the security and social position it provided. "At the bottom of all that an American does," said a shrewd foreign commentator, "is money; beneath every word, money." Perhaps this was the substitute they found for all that had been lost from that earlier and simpler time when men were content to stay close to the place where they were born.

The second basic quality about these Americans was that they were champions of equality—that is, of course, for those who were white and male. Women did not need equality. They were up there on their pedestals shining forth beauty and goodness. To give them equality would demean their status in society. So the poor unfortunate female had no rights. She was chattel. She could not vote or hold office; her "right" to property was limited; she could not enter most professions; she could not make a will, sign a contract, or witness a deed without her father's or husband's consent; and her children could be taken from her if her husband so directed. Nor was there any concerted drive for equality for blacks or Indians on the part of most Americans. Women, blacks, and Indians just didn't enter the thinking of these people when they argued for equality.

To fault Americans of this period for failing to understand what the modern world means by equality is a pointless and futile exercise. But if they are examined on their own terms, with all their faults and limitations, they make an exciting bunch to watch as they changed their world and shaped so many things that became basic to the American system. Not all they attempted can be described here. The list is much too long. The efforts to achieve women's rights; the temperance and peace movements; the reforms of education, penal institutions, and insane asylums; the religious innovations; the search for perfection in communal living—all these are far too complex and involved to discuss in a short book. Besides, these reform movements expressed the thinking and activity of a relatively small number of Americans. They were not typical. What will be attempted here is a discussion of the *political* issues of the Jacksonian age—those which had a major impact on the history of the country or still maintain their relevance today. These issues include the problem of keeping the relatively new Union in one piece despite sectional arguments, especially over slavery; the push toward a more democratic society; the problem of the Indian presence in the midst of a white society; the growth of the power of the presidency; and the changing structure and operation of the federal government as controlled by the emergent two-party system.

And central to all these issues—the one person around whom much of the controversy of this era raged—was Andrew Jackson.

Jackson's name still clangs with the sound of battle. Disagreement over his accomplishments and contributions persists to this day. Here was the man whose election to the presidency his contemporaries considered the mark of a new era in American politics. That era was later termed "the rise of the common man." For with the widespread removal of restrictions to the suffrage, the electorate trooped to the polls and chose this westerner as their President, a man who had not only risen from poverty to fortune on the frontier but also gained undying fame in the War of 1812 as the conqueror of the British invaders.

Jackson was both a product and shaper of his age. He was the living embodiment of the changes and improvements that had occurred in the country since the Revolution. He was the symbol of the aspirations and expectations of Americans committed to "go ahead" and the creation of a more equal and democratic society. He was simply "the Hero," the man whose military victories restored the nation's confidence in its ability to face a hostile world and proudly—defiantly—proclaim its liberty and independence.

Andrew Jackson was the nation's image of itself.

2

Andrew Jackson

THE LIFE OF Andrew Jackson spanned the years in which the nation moved from colonial status to an independent, bustling, thriving republic, just emerging as an industrial society, sure of itself and its future, and chewing up a continent as fast as Americans could clear it of Indians, Mexicans, Spaniards, Englishmen, and any others in their way. Jackson's life began in poverty and ended in unparalleled success and triumph. It was a life that epitomized what would later be called the "American dream." He was a "self-made man"—to use a term invented at this time—who through his own efforts and talents climbed from obscurity to the rank of first citizen in the nation.

Andrew Jackson was born on March 15, 1767, in the Waxhaw settlement on the northern South Carolina frontier, a remote community on the rim of civilized life. His father had migrated with his wife from Carrickfergus in northern Ireland, and died shortly before Andrew was born. During the American Revolution his mother died of cholera while nursing patriot soldiers held captive aboard British prison ships in Charleston harbor, and his two older brothers also died during the Revolution, their deaths indirectly connected to the war. Orphaned at the age of fourteen, Andrew drifted from place to place and one occupation to another, including schoolteaching and saddlemaking. In these early years he gained a reputation for a fiery temper, easily ignited by a thoughtless word or hostile glance. Frequently he was sullen, depressed, and angry—no doubt because he felt alone in the world. For a time he led a wild life, drinking, gambling, mischief-making. When he was seventeen he decided that he would become a lawyer, since that occupation offered the best opportunity for a young man anxious to make his fortune and place his mark on the world.

So off Jackson went to North Carolina, to a town seventy-five miles from the Waxhaw settlement called Salisbury, where he entered the law office of Spruce McCay. For two years he prepared himself for admission to the bar by "reading law" with McCay and making himself generally useful around the office by copying papers, running errands, and cleaning the rooms. Not that his serious purpose tamed his wild spirits. "Andrew Jackson," said one man, "was the most roaring, rollicking, game-cocking, horse-racing, card-playing, mischievous fellow, that ever lived in Salisbury." Years later when the sober-minded people of Salisbury heard that Jackson was running for the presidency, they were appalled. "What?" cried one woman. "Jackson up for the President? *Jackson? Andrew* Jackson? The Jackson that used to live in Salisbury? Why, when he was here, he was such a rake that my husband would not bring him into the house! It is true, he *might* have taken him out to the stable to weigh horses for a race, and might drink a glass of whiskey with him *there*. Well, if Andrew Jackson can be President, anybody can!"

Nevertheless, he learned the law, enough of it at any rate to be certified by two judges on September 26, 1787. The judges said Jackson was a man of "unblemished" moral character and in their judgment would not dishonor the profession. Reckoning that his best opportunity and hope for future success lay west of the Alleghenies, Jackson packed a few belongings, a gun, and a wallet containing letters of introduction, and headed west. He did not get very far when he ran into trouble. At Jonesboro he fought his first known duel. Apparently the other man made some sarcastic remark about Jackson's legal ability. In any event no one was hurt in the duel and Jackson's honor was restored.

All his life Jackson suffered from a violent temper, although after he married, his wife helped him to bring it under control. But when it exploded, it terrified everyone within the sound of his voice. He could flood a room with the sounds of God's wrath, roaring and lashing at those who had triggered the explosion. During these convulsions his deep blue eyes blazed with such passion that observers feared he would burst a blood vessel and bring on a stroke. Yet those who really knew him later claimed that most of these tantrums were faked in order to intimidate people and get what he wanted, that even during the height of a great passion when he was screaming and threatening, he was in absolute control of himself. "No man knew better than Andrew Jackson," wrote one man, "when to get into a passion and when not." Because he was so good at these performances, he found they were useful in dealing with men and bending them to his will, especially politicians.

In 1788, when he was twenty-one, Jackson arrived in Nashville, where he met Rachel Donelson Robards. Her family had been among the first settlers of Tennessee. Unfortunately, when Jackson met Rachel she was already married to Lewis Robards, a man pathologically suspicious of every move his wife made. Eventually, when she could stand the suspicion and quarrels no longer, she ran away from him. And Jackson went with her—for protection, he later said. Then Rachel, after waiting several months to give Robards enough time to obtain a divorce, married Jackson.

It was a mistake. There had been no divorce, although Rachel and Andrew thought there had, and for two years she was technically a bigamist. Later, on January 17, 1794, after Robards had in fact obtained a divorce on grounds of desertion and adultery, she "remarried" Jackson. These unfortunate circumstances caused much sorrow and trouble for the couple, particularly in later years when Jackson emerged as a presidential candidate and his political enemies thought they could injure him by splattering the details of the marriage in the public prints.

Sensitive to the point of violence about the circumstances of his marriage, Jackson fought several duels with men who let slip some stupid or vicious remark. He fought his most famous duel in 1806 with Charles Dickinson, a young neighbor who had a reputation as the "best shot in Tennessee." The immediate cause of the gunfight was a disagreement over a horse-race wager, but Dickinson had made some derogatory comment about the marriage while drinking in a tavern. He had taken Rachel's "sacred name" into his "polluted mouth," and Jackson demanded satisfaction.

The two men met with their seconds and surgeons on a lovely late

May day in 1806 in a poplar forest near a river bottom not far from Nashville. "How do you feel about it now?" Jackson was asked by one member of his party.

"Oh, all right," came the reply. "I shall wing him, never fear."

Eight paces were measured off and the two men took their places facing one another. "Are you ready?" asked John Overton, Jackson's second and his oldest friend in Tennessee.

"I am ready," replied Dickinson.

"I am ready," responded Jackson.

"Fire!" cried Overton.

Dickinson quickly raised his pistol and fired. The ball struck Jackson directly in the chest, causing a puff of dust to rise from Jackson's coat.

"He is surely hit," thought Overton, "and in a bad place, too." But Jackson did not fall. In fact he hardly moved. He stood perfectly still, then slowly raised his left arm and pressed it tightly against his throbbing chest. "Erect and grim as Fate he stood," wrote an observer, "his teeth clenched, raising his pistol."

Aghast to see his enemy still standing, Dickinson cried out, "Great God! have I missed him?" As he spoke Dickinson stepped back two paces, leaving the mark and thereby violating the dueling code since it was tantamount to running away.

"Back to the MARK, sir!" called Overton, his hand on his own pistol ready to shoot Dickinson, as the code directed, if he failed to respond.

Dickinson realized what he had unconsciously done and immediately returned to his proper position. He had to stand there and wait, sweating out each moment until Jackson returned the fire.

Raising his gun and taking careful aim, Jackson squeezed the trigger. With a *click* the hammer sprang forward but stopped at the half-cocked position. Jackson drew the hammer back again and aimed a second time; all the while Dickinson just stood there, his entire body tensed to receive the shot.

Jackson fired. The bullet tore through Dickinson's body a trifle below the rib cage. Dickinson's face paled, he swayed slightly and then slumped forward. His friends rushed to his aid and gently seated him on the ground. They stripped away some of his clothes. His trousers reddened. Blood gushed from his side. There was nothing anyone could do, and Dickinson slowly bled to death.

Overton walked over to Jackson and told him what had happened. As the two men walked away the surgeon joined them and noticed that one of Jackson's shoes was full of blood. A quick examination showed that Jackson had suffered a broken rib, possibly two. Dickinson had aimed well, but Jackson's loose-fitting coat, buttoned over the chest, had saved his life. Because of it Dickinson had misjudged his target. He aimed for the heart but struck a rib instead.

"But I should have hit him if he had shot me through the brain," was Jackson's final comment.

That last remark says something about Jackson's character—how fierce his resolution when he had set his mind on a particular object. He willed himself to stay alive and kill Dickinson. In the future, even though his body throbbed with pain because of his several wounds and ailments picked up fighting Indians and British soldiers, he willed himself to keep going, to fight on, to pursue his goals. Later, as President, he repeatedly faced political enemies who maneuvered to thwart his intentions or cripple his legislative goals. Even when he lay prostrated in his bed, his lungs bleeding because of his ancient wounds, his eyes glowed with determination to "go ahead" and fight through to political victory.

Despite his marriage problem, Jackson prospered as a lawyer and planter. Indeed, his marriage was very advantageous to him, for he had allied himself with one of the leading families of Tennessee.

When Jackson had first arrived in Nashville he had been appointed public prosecutor, and he established his reputation for law enforcement almost overnight. He enforced seventy writs against delinquent debtors in his first month on the job. Naturally his conscientious performance of duty infuriated some of the debtors. One of them walked up to Jackson one day and to show his anger deliberately stepped on the young man's foot. Calmly, Jackson turned around, picked up a piece of wood, and knocked the man out cold. There was no fooling around with Andrew Jackson.

His career moved steadily ahead. He was elected to the convention that wrote Tennessee's constitution. He was the state's first representative to the United States Congress, and in 1797 was elected to the U.S. Senate. Later he was appointed a judge of the Superior Court of Tennessee.

When the War of 1812 broke out Jackson happened to be Major General of the Tennessee militia. It was sheer luck. He was the General by virtue of nothing more than his election by the militiamen. Despite his lack of military training or experience, he quickly proved himself an excellent general because of his natural qualities of leadership. Soldiers respected him. They knew he was tough and brave, and they trusted him.

Ordered to subdue the Creek Indians who had attacked settlers along the Alabama frontier, Jackson crushed them in a series of splendidly executed military engagements and then imposed a treaty that forever destroyed their power to menace the United States. In admiration and affection his soldiers began calling him "Old Hickory," because hickory was the toughest wood they knew.

Still, it was not his reputation for killing Indians that launched Jackson's national career and reputation; it was his phenomenal victory over the British at New Orleans during the War of 1812. The nation had gone to war with England, not simply to redress such grievances as British seizure of American ships and impressment of American sailors, but to prove to itself that it could safeguard its independence and freedom against all European hostility, especially England's. But the war turned out to be one unmitigated military disaster after another for Americans. It brought into question the United States' capacity to defend its independence. The war seemed to nullify the fruits of the American Revolution. Profound despair gripped the nation.

Then came the Battle of New Orleans. On January 8, 1815, Jackson, with an army of volunteers from most of the Western states plus blacks and pirates, smashed a British army attempting to invade the country from the Gulf of Mexico. Over two thousand invading soldiers were killed or wounded, while less than a dozen Americans fell before British guns. It was a fantastic victory. Britain, the conqueror of Napoleon, the colossus of western Europe, had sustained a crushing military defeat at the hands of American sharpshooters and cannoneers. This single battle confirmed to the world—or so Americans claimed—that the United States could defend and protect the freedom it had won just a few decades earlier. Europe might sneer at American independence and Britain assault it, but Jackson—"by God"—taught them to respect it.

From the moment they heard about the victory, and its dimensions in terms of men killed and wounded, Americans idolized Andrew Jackson. He had restored their pride in themselves and in their nation. He had renewed their self-confidence. So, said one writer, you can talk about Columbus, Benjamin Franklin, Washington, and Jefferson and all they had accomplished; you can talk about fifty years of democratic government, a free press, and free schools, about a country whose population had quadrupled and its resources multiplied tenfold—but what did it all add up to? The "result of all was," he said, "that the people of the United States had arrived at the capacity of honoring Andrew Jackson before all other living men."

Now nothing was too good for him. No praise too extravagant. No honor too lavish. He was the Hero.

Jackson added to his fame and the nation's further glory when, in 1818, he invaded eastern Florida, which was still held by the Spanish, in order to stop frontier attacks by Seminole Indians. He defeated the Indians, drove out the Spanish, and seized control of Florida. Again it was a stunning performance, and although his actions provoked an international furor and almost precipitated a war with Spain, they ultimately led to the formal and legal acquisition of Florida by the United States. The treaty that arranged the transfer of ownership also provided that Spain surrender its claims in the extreme Northwest called the Oregon country, thus catapulting the United States into a trans-continental power. What had begun as a series of settlements along the Atlantic shore in the seventeenth century now in the nineteenth century stretched three thousand miles from ocean to ocean.

The American people could never do enough for Andrew Jackson. He had their devotion, their trust, their love. So, a few years later, they raised him to the presidency, accepting his leadership in 1828 as testament to their profound faith in his capacity to govern and guide the nation. Of course there were some who questioned military prowess as a qualification for the presidency. They supported the reelection of the incumbent, John Quincy Adams. Senators Henry Clay of Kentucky and Daniel Webster of Massachusetts were two such men. They agreed the Hero could kill Indians and invading foreigners rather handsomely but doubted he was presidential material. Clay called him a "military chieftain" and worried for the safety of the country under his direction. After all, Jackson had a very limited education, and nothing in his civilian career, according to Clay, indicated a capacity or ability to administer the government.

But Jackson was different from ordinary men, protested his supporters. It wasn't his military career alone that made him stand apart. Not any one thing, really. "One must not separate his talents . . ." wrote a contemporary, "but take the tout ensemble of the man, and I venture to say there is not such another in the United States. . . . History is sure to preserve the name of any man who has had the strength and

25

Engraved by Geo. T... from a painting by Jarvis, taken from life 1815,
now in the Possession of Jonathan Hunt Esq.

Andrew Jackson

This engraving of Andrew Jackson was made from a portrait painted in New
Orleans in 1815, at the time of Jackson's military triumph. A reasonably good
likeness, except for the Napoleonic hair swirls.

genius to stamp his own character on the people over whose destinies he presided.'' By his election as President of the United States in 1828, Andrew Jackson seemed a living symbol of the advance of American democracy.

Jackson's election, expressed by more than half a million of his fellow citizens, was his greatest triumph. But it came at the very moment of his greatest personal tragedy. He had not yet taken office. He was home in Tennessee, living at his plantation—Jackson had no pretensions, and called it his farm—just outside Nashville. It was a December day and all were going about their business in the usual way. Jackson was in the fields overseeing the work of his slaves. His wife Rachel—whom he had idolized probably from the moment he laid eyes on her—scurried about the large house, which Jackson called the Hermitage, supervising the duties of her servants. Rachel was a heavyset and dark-complexioned woman, pious and charitable, who loved to sit in her rocker and smoke her pipe and listen to her husband recount his many adventures. Everyone called her ''Aunt Rachel.'' That's how affectionate they felt toward her.

On this particular day Old Hannah, one of the house slaves, asked Rachel to come into the kitchen to give advice about the preparation of the evening meal. Rachel explained what she wanted to the cook and then returned to the sitting room. Suddenly, she stopped in her tracks. She clutched her heart and let out a scream. Sinking into a chair, she struggled for breath, falling forward into Hannah's arms. Servants came running when they heard the scream and lifted Rachel gently onto her bed. Hannah tried to apply the only remedy she knew. She vigorously rubbed her mistress's side ''till it was black and blue.''

Still no relief. The stricken woman writhed in agony. She gasped for breath. She twisted and turned, clutching the bed sheets as she groped for release from the pain.

When Jackson heard what was happening he came running from the fields, ''his face lined with alarm beyond description.'' A niece hurried in from her house nearby. Soon the Hermitage was filled with relatives, friends, and servants, all trying to be helpful but all incapable of doing anything useful. The doctor finally arrived and did what he could to make her comfortable. For the next few days Rachel suffered great pain. During this time Jackson left her side for only ten minutes.

Rachel survived the first onslaught of a massive heart attack. Within two days she was feeling a trifle better; the intense pain had subsided and

27

she could breathe with less difficulty. She begged her husband to leave her and get some sleep himself. But Jackson refused; he distrusted her reassuring words.

Over the next several days Rachel continued to improve. She was now free from pain, although she was weak and listless. Jackson stayed with her, watching, praying. By Monday, December 23, Rachel appeared so much better that she finally talked the General into lying on a sofa in the adjoining room to get a few hours' sleep. The doctor remained in the house and there were servants watching Rachel's every move. It seemed at last that Jackson could safely leave her.

It was nine P.M. Jackson kissed his wife and retired to the next room, removing his coat. He was gone only five minutes. The servants lifted Rachel from her bed so that the sheets could be arranged and smoothed for the night. While sitting in the chair, supported by Hannah, Rachel suffered a second attack. She let out a long, loud cry. There was a "rattling sound in her throat." Her head fell forward and she never spoke or breathed again.

Jackson raced into the room when he heard the cry. The doctor, relatives, and servants rushed in, too. Rachel was quickly returned to her bed. The doctor listened for life.

Jackson, almost beside himself with fear, searched the doctor's face to catch some knowledge of his wife's condition.

"Bleed her," he commanded.

The doctor opened her arm, but no blood flowed.

Jackson froze.

"Try the temple, Doctor," he pleaded.

Again the doctor cut into her flesh. Two drops oozed from the incision and stained her cap. That was all.

Her husband refused to believe that Rachel Jackson was dead. For hours he stared intently into her face, hoping to see signs of returning life. Not until she grew cold did he accept the truth that his beloved was gone.

The servants then prepared a table "for laying her out." His voice choking, Jackson said to them, "Spread four blankets upon it. If she comes to, she will not lie so hard upon the table."

The body was arranged and Jackson spent the night by Rachel's side, his face in his hands, grieving. Once in a while he would look into the face and feel the heart and pulse of the one person to whom he was totally and utterly devoted.

A friend arrived the next day and found Jackson still sitting there. He was wholly inconsolable. He had quite lost his voice. He sat in the room nearly all the next day, only stirring a little to sip some coffee which was pressed on him by his friend.

On Christmas Eve, 1828, Rachel Jackson was buried in her garden just a few hundred yards from the Hermitage mansion. Ten thousand people came for the funeral, double the population of Nashville. In part it was a tribute to a woman known for her charity and gentleness; in larger part it was a salute to her husband, to whom they wished to demonstrate their affection.

Jackson, bowed down with grief, was helped to the graveside by two army friends. "I never pitied any person more in my life," wrote one man. "I shall never forget his look of grief."

Jackson never fully recovered from the shock of Rachel's death. As far as he was concerned, she had been murdered by those vile "pander heads," as he called them, who had slandered her as a bigamist and adultress during the election. They drove her to her grave, he said. "May God Almighty forgive her murderers as I know she forgave them," he wrote. "I never can."

Jackson's friends urged him to think about his responsibilities as President. There was the inauguration ahead; there were plans to be formulated for the commencement of his administration. But he remained inconsolable, just sitting in the Hermitage, hardly stirring himself to acknowledge the presence or questions of his friends. "My heart is nearly broke," he wrote as he finally summoned the strength and will to pack and leave for Washington.

On January 18, 1829—almost a month to the day after Rachel's initial attack—Jackson boarded a steamboat to begin the long journey to the nation's capital to assume his presidency. As his boat ascended the river, other vessels, crowded with people, circled around, serving as a kind of escort. People standing on the decks called to Jackson, shouting their cheers. Each time he heard the salute the President-elect came out on deck and returned the greeting by tipping his hat. What a democrat, the crowd agreed, truly a man of the people. What previous President would have responded so instinctively and so graciously? Clearly, Jackson's election marked a new beginning in the relationship between the government and the people.

The Hero arrived in Washington early in February to begin arranging some of the details required by his imminent inauguration. For the most

Jackson en route to his Washington inauguration, suggesting the easy and natural rapport he had with the immense crowds who greeted him.

part Jackson kept out of sight for the next few weeks, trying to avoid a popular demonstration to acknowledge his presence. But that did not keep the people and his party from standing witness to his inauguration as President on March 4, 1829.

By the thousands they came, mobbing the capital "like the inundation of the northern barbarians into Rome," sniffed Senator Daniel Webster. And they came from every part of the country and represented every walk of life—farmers, mechanics, merchants, frontiersmen, city dwellers. "I never saw such a crowd here before," said Webster. "Persons have come five hundred miles to see General Jackson, *and they really seem to think that the country is rescued from some danger!*"

Twenty thousand people swarmed through the streets and avenues of Washington on inauguration day. They headed for the Capitol, where on the east portico Jackson would recite the oath of office and read his inaugural address. The day was bright and balmy, one of those magnificent spring days that Washington sometimes enjoys in early March. Around the Capitol building and into the square in front of the east portico people gathered "like a great agitated sea," moving, jumping up and down, shoving and pushing, anxious for the ceremonies to begin. Some of them swept up the long portico stairs to get a better position but were stopped by a ship's cable that was stretched across the stairs, two-thirds of the way from the bottom. After what seemed like an interminable delay the doors of the rotunda finally opened. Marshals marched out looking dignified and solemn, followed by the judges of the Supreme Court of the United States.

Then the people saw Jackson emerging from between the columns of the portico. They started shouting, waving, and clapping their hands. "Hurray! Hurray! Hurray!" they cried.

"Never can I forget the spectacle," said one man, "nor the electrifying moment when the eager, expectant eyes of that vast and motley multitude caught sight . . . of their adored leader." In an instant, as if by "magic," the color of the whole mass changed—"all hats were off at once, and the dark tint which usually pervades a mixed map of men was turned . . . into the bright hue of ten thousand upturned and exultant human faces, radiant with sudden joy." Jackson stared for a moment at this ecstatic mass of humanity, and then in a gesture that thrilled the crowd, he bowed low before them. He bowed to the "majesty of the people."

Jackson looked very dignified, very impressive. In fact Mrs. Daniel Webster, who was no great admirer of the Hero, had to admit that he was

31

the most "presidential looking" of all the recent candidates for chief executive, and that included men like incumbent President John Quincy Adams, Henry Clay of Kentucky, John C. Calhoun of South Carolina, and William H. Crawford of Georgia. At the time of his inauguration Jackson was nearly sixty-two years old. Tall and cadaverously thin, he carried himself with military stiffness. His face was long, with a sharp jaw, and lighted by clear blue eyes. His short gray-white hair bristled and stood almost as erect as the President-elect himself.

As Jackson stared down on the sea of faces before him cannons began booming from Alexandria and Fort Warburton to punctuate the solemnity of the moment. He then turned to read his inaugural speech and the crowd hushed to hear his words. As Margaret Bayard Smith, the very intelligent and aristocratic wife of the Senator from Maryland, said: "It was an almost breathless silence." Francis Scott Key, author of "The Star Spangled Banner," gaped at this singular spectacle unfolding before his eyes. "It is beautiful," he gasped, "it is sublime!"

Jackson began to speak. "Fellow-citizens," he said in a near whisper. "About to undertake the arduous duties that I have been appointed to perform by the choice of a free people, I avail of this . . . solemn occasion to express [my] gratitude." But Jackson's voice did not carry very well in this outdoor arena and so only those nearest to him heard his words. Fortunately, the speech was short, lasting hardly ten minutes. Among a number of things, he said he hoped to extinguish the national debt as well as safeguard the rights of the states. But what was most important to him, he declared, was "the task of *reform*, which will require particularly the correction of those abuses that have brought the patronage of the Federal Government into conflict with the freedom of elections . . . [or] have placed or continued power in unfaithful or incompetent hands."

When Jackson finished his prepared speech Chief Justice John Marshall stepped forward and administered the oath of office. That done, Jackson took the Bible from the marshal who held it during the oath taking, pressed it to his lips, laid it down reverently and then bowed again to the people. "Yes," said the haughty Mrs. Smith, "to the people in all their majesty."

The crowd could no longer restrain itself. The people charged forward, broke the chain barring their way, and swarmed around the President, reaching out and clutching his hand to shake it. Only with difficulty did Jackson escape back through the Capitol and down the hill to the gateway that opened to the long avenue leading to the White

House. Here again the new President was stopped by a "living mass" that was "impenetrable." After a time some friends forced an opening through the crowd so that Jackson could reach the horse which had been provided for his journey to the executive mansion. As the Hero mounted, the crowd let out a shout. Everything he did seemed to please them. Then, slowly, he headed for the White House, and oh, said Mrs. Smith, "such a cortege as followed him! Country men, farmers, gentlemen, mounted and dismounted, boys, women and children, black and white. Carriages, wagons and carts all pursuing him to the President's house." People standing at the upper windows of their homes cheered the President as he rode by. As usual, Jackson responded by tipping his hat.

Never had there been such an inauguration of a President. Never before had the ordinary citizen—the common man—so spontaneously expressed his enthusiasm for a new administration. When Thomas Jefferson was inaugurated chief executive twenty-eight years earlier he simply walked from his boardinghouse to the Capitol, was sworn in, and then walked back and joined his messmates at the boardinghouse for lunch. But here was Jackson riding toward the White House with an enormous mob in tow. It suddenly occurred to a number of gentlemen and ladies who were watching the procession from the safety of their homes that this motley crew of farmers, workers, boys, women, children, and lord-knows-what-else were intending to enter the "President's palace," as they grandly termed the White House. The "palace" was about to be invaded by the masses, the rabble. People from "the highest and most polished," said Joseph Story, the learned jurist, now an Associate Justice of the Supreme Court, "down to the most vulgar and gross in the nation" poured into the executive mansion. Hundreds of them by the minute jammed their way through every door of the building. "I never saw such a mixture," moaned Story. Most of them were common, ordinary people. "The reign of KING MOB seemed triumphant," he said. "I was glad to escape from the scene as soon as possible."

When Mrs. Smith and her family arrived at the White House they were aghast at the spectacle taking place in the "palace." "What a scene did we witness!" she wrote. "*The Majesty of the People* had disappeared, and a rabble, a mob, of boys, negros [*sic*], women, children, scrambling, fighting, romping. What a pity what a pity."

A modest reception in the White House had been planned; what occurred was shocking to those used to "elitist" republicanism. Barrels

14918

of orange punch had been prepared, but as the waiters opened the doors to carry them out, the mob rushed forward to seize them. The punch splashed on the carpets as waiters and guests collided. Glasses fell to the floor and were stepped on; pails of liquor were overturned; "and the most painful confusion prevailed." It was mortifying, said one observer, to see men "with boots heavy with mud, standing on the damask satin covered chairs," just to catch sight of the President.

And poor Jackson. They nearly killed him. He was, said Mrs. Smith, "*literally* nearly pressed to death and almost suffocated and torn to pieces in their eagerness to shake hands with Old Hickory." Finally the pressure got so bad and the danger of actually injuring the President became so real that a number of men formed a ring around him and led him to a back entrance so he could escape the dangerous exuberance of the people and return to his temporary lodgings at Gatsby's Hotel.

But the President's disappearance did not dampen the mood of the celebrants. The mayhem, if anything, got worse. Cut glass and china worth several thousand dollars was smashed in the struggle to find refreshments. Ladies fainted. Men were seen with bloody noses. At last someone got the bright idea of removing the liquor and ice cream into the garden. As the refreshments disappeared outside, men and boys jumped through the windows to get to them.

Just in time, breathed Mrs. Smith with relief. The house could not have survived the pressure much longer—to say nothing of the furnishings. "We had a regular Saturnalia," laughed one Congressman who witnessed the rampage and described it to a friend. The mob, he wrote, was "one uninterrupted stream of mud and filth."

Ladies like Mrs. Smith and gentlemen like Justice Story had come to the White House expecting a levee, such as those calm, slightly aristocratic receptions that had honored the presidencies of George Washington, John and John Quincy Adams, James Madison, and James Monroe. But instead they found people gathered *en masse*, joyously, raucously, destructively celebrating the inauguration of their Hero.

"It was the People's day, and the People's President, and the People shall rule." That was the sum and substance of it, according to most contemporaries. It was the end of limited republicanism, established under the Constitution, restricting government to the few—the educated, the wellborn, the property owners. Here was the beginning of truly popular government in America—at least in spirit. And for the next eight years, under the administration of President Andrew Jackson, that spirit, in several particulars, was translated into political reality.

3

The Democratic Party

THE EMERGENCE OF a truly democratic, popular government did not happen just because the people willed it. Nor was it a simple process of evolution going back to colonial times and stimulated by the doctrines of the Declaration of Independence, the Revolution, or the genius of the Constitution. To a large extent, popular government emerged because a relatively small group of men engineered it. These men were gifted politicians. They were outstanding public officials, and the most prominent included men of varying political opinions such as Martin Van Buren of New York, Henry Clay of Kentucky, Daniel Webster of Massachusetts, Thomas Hart Benton of Missouri and John C. Calhoun of South Carolina.

To understand the contribution made to democratic government during the Jacksonian era it is necessary to look back prior to Jackson's election, back to the beginning of the nineteenth century, back to the early days of the Republic. Two developments triggered the democratic changes that occurred during the Jacksonian years. The first was the broadening of the franchise. In the preceding three decades the states had steadily eliminated restrictions on voting, so that by 1828 a great many white males over twenty-one enjoyed the right of the ballot.

Because they enjoyed this right did not necessarily mean they would exercise it. Frequently—more times than not—they had to be urged and courted and cajoled into exercising it. "Our old way of conducting elections," wrote one politician in Illinois, "required each aspirant for office to announce himself as a candidate." Then he traveled around the state, making speeches, conversing with the electorate, soliciting votes, and "whispering slanders" against his opponents. Now, with a greater number of people enfranchised, it was necessary to devise "new modes" of soliciting and concentrating and controlling voter participation. This new situation encouraged skillful, ambitious, and intelligent politicians to invent ways to involve and manage the mass electorate. Eventually they succeeded, and their success constituted a radically transformed electoral process. The process was democratized.

The second development was the emergence of political parties in America. From the beginning the leaders of the new American nation had expressed a deep horror of political parties, calling them cabals of willful men devoted to their own selfish purposes and not the good of the general public. George Washington said parties were instruments of dissention and discord, and John Adams declared that the "division of the republic into two great parties . . . is to be dreaded as the greatest political evil under our Constitution."

Despite these fears and warnings, a two-party system developed within a few years of Washington's inauguration as first President. Washington had brought into his Cabinet two highly intelligent, individual, and opinionated men who fundamentally disagreed on the direction the government should take and set about competing with one another to gain a commitment from Washington to their point of view. Thomas Jefferson as Secretary of State and Alexander Hamilton as Secretary of the Treasury represented two conflicting philosophies of government. Hamilton insisted on wide powers for the federal government in order to inaugurate an economic program that, by uniting private interest to public duty, would produce a strong and efficient national economy. He understood that only a government which guaranteed the financial interests of its constituency was likely to succeed. Jefferson, on the other hand, took exception to Hamilton's concept of expanding federal power. He emphasized the need and value of local autonomy in order to preserve individual freedom.

The two-party system which began to emerge was the best thing that could have happened to the country. Most Americans were (and still are)

36

essentially conservative in their politics. As a matter of fact no genuinely radical ideas or parties have ever taken deep root in the nation. Even so, Americans demand change, although they abhor revolution. Thus, with a two-party system as it developed, change could be achieved through normal shifts in government administration from one party to another, all obtained in regular elections through nonviolent party contest.

The fears of Washington and other Founding Fathers about parties slowly changed during the first decades of the nineteenth century. But the really big change came during the Jacksonian age with the appearance of a new breed of professional politician. Men like Van Buren, Clay, and others lacked the accomplishments of the statesmen of the Revolutionary generation. They could not match their careers against those of statesmen such as Washington, Jefferson, Hamilton, Madison, and dozens of others who had won the Revolution, written or signed the Declaration, framed the Constitution, or adopted constitutions for their states. When the politicians of this second generation came before the American people and asked for votes, they could not offer the kind of distinction and accomplishment that the first generation had provided. So, lacking extraordinary credentials, they were forced to rely on the party system to advance their ideas and careers. Ambitious for the offices once occupied by the Founding Fathers, who were dead or fast dying off by this time, they shrewdly recognized party organization as the best means of gaining their objectives. Not surprisingly, they praised the party system as the surest safeguard for a free and representative government. Modern government, they contended, demanded well-functioning political parties openly arrayed against each other. Parties preserved liberty by allowing for organized opposition. They would inhibit governmental corruption by providing periodic reexamination of the conduct of public business at election time. In sum, these men argued, democratic principles in government were impossible without party politics.

Thus, within a forty-year period, from the founding of the republic under the Constitution to the Age of Jackson, political thinking had shifted from viewing parties as destructive instruments to seeing them as essential to democratic government.

These second-generation politicians—the Van Burens, Clays, Websters, and hundreds of others—quickly became professional in the art of politics. It was their business to win elections; they had to depend on their skill as organizers, as speakers, and as managers to capture the support of the American voter. They were men of uncommon ability in one or another endeavor. A few of them were outstanding public speakers; others, intrepid organizers or managers. One was a profound political theoretician. Many were outstanding statesmen, men of high principle, committed to popular government and individual freedom. They supported either the Jeffersonian doctrine, which urged limiting governmental power, or the Hamiltonian position of expanding the central government to assist the progress and prosperity of the entire nation. But in these early Jacksonian years all of them actively engaged in restructuring the two major parties to modernize their operation. Their activities in party politics will be emphasized here, rather than their individual philosophies or principles of government, because these activities had much to do with advancing democracy within the American nation.

Perhaps Martin Van Buren was the most typical and most successful of this new breed of politician. Known as the "Little Magician" or "Red Fox of Kinderhook" because of his extraordinary skill as a political manager, Van Buren, over the years, built a political organization in New York known as the "Albany Regency" to run the political business of the state while he was absent in Washington. This was one of the first statewide political machines in the United States. It had a governing council set up in Albany consisting of some of the state's best political talents, including William L. Marcy, Silas Wright, Jr., Azariah C. Flagg, Benjamin F. Butler, and Edwin Croswell, editor of the *Albany Argus*, the party's newspaper mouthpiece.

Two of these men became United States Senators, two became Governors of the state, one might have become President of the United States except that he died before the convention could nominate him, another won appointment as United States Attorney General, and still another became Secretary of State. All obviously men of talent. With control of the state legislature, the Regency directed the political affairs of New York, encouraging young lawyers and newspapermen in the state to accept Regency leadership and seek advancement in elective office through its sponsorship and support. It devised and invented means for keeping the electorate loyal to the party and regular in its voting. Through the *Albany Argus* it informed the faithful of the party line.

Van Buren was born in Kinderhook, New York, on December 5, 1782—just a year after the nation had won its independence. He was the son of a tavern keeper, and through hard work and native intelligence he learned enough law as a clerk in several law offices to be licensed to practice within the state. Thereafter his rise to political prominence was swift. He had learned his politics in his father's tavern. He had learned how to influence men, how to talk with them, how to win their confidence. First he was appointed fence-viewer, then Surrogate of Columbia County; subsequently he was elected state senator, state attorney general, and then United States Senator.

Van Buren was a short man, probably no taller than five feet four and a half inches, which explains why it was not enough to call him a "Magician." It had to be "Little Magician." (And it says something about the new style of politics during this Jacksonian age that all the Presidents of both parties, beginning with the Hero in 1828, had nicknames: Jackson was the Hero or Old Hickory; Van Buren, elected in 1836, was the Little Magician; then came Tippecanoe and Tyler, Too, otherwise known as William Henry Harrison and John Tyler; James Knox Polk was Young Hickory, elected in 1844; and finally, in 1848, Zachary Taylor was called Old Rough and Ready. The six Presidents who preceded Jackson never had such nicknames. The democratization of the presidency obviously included some inelegant side effects.)

Van Buren was fair-complexioned with light, sandy-colored hair and "small brilliant eyes" under a bulging forehead. Most people, except of course his enemies, thought he was one of the most charming men of his age. Men and women vied for his company because he was friendly, urbane, and gracious, and his conversation "rich in information." He was courteous to all, perhaps overly so. He never showed what he was really thinking. He was very discreet, very guarded, very careful in everything he said and did. Consequently, he was frequently accused of being "non-committal" on most important political issues. There was a story repeatedly told about him that illustrates the point. He was giving a speech in Albany on the tariff question, a touchy if not dangerous issue. When he finished there was a great burst of applause. One man in the audience supposedly turned to his friend, Mr. Benjamin Knower.

"Mr. Knower!" he said, "that was a very able speech."

"Yes, very able," came the reply.

"Mr. Knower! on which side of the Tariff question was it?"

"That is the very point I was thinking about when you first spoke to me," answered the puzzled Knower.

Van Buren was more a manager of men than a public speaker,

None of the paintings or photographs of Van Buren do him justice. That none convey his charm, graciousness and urbanity, or his political shrewdness and cunning, may itself say something about his character.

operating quietly but with great force and persuasion. He did not have the oratorical flair of a Daniel Webster or the easy speaking style of a Henry Clay, so his influence was felt more behind the scenes. Which explains why some men were very distrustful of him, why when any peculiar circumstances or untoward developments occurred they were sure to see "Mr. Van Buren's sly hand" in them.

As a shrewd observer of the political scene, as an astute judge of men, Van Buren understood the meaning of Andrew Jackson's enormous popularity with the American people long before the election of 1828. He also appreciated what it might mean to his own political ambitions if he could catch hold of Jackson's long coattails. But Van Buren was not a political hack, limited simply to the gratification of his electoral ambition. He recognized that with Jackson he might help direct the country, and the party gathered behind him, along lines compatible with his philosophy of government—a philosophy he claimed was based on the principles and doctrines of Thomas Jefferson. Intellectually, like Jefferson, Van Buren was committed to the doctrine of states' rights, namely that those powers not expressly delegated by the Constitution to the federal government were reserved to the states and the people. He vigorously opposed a strong central government in Washington; he believed in rigid economy when budgeting national expenditures; and he tended to oppose tariffs and public works sponsored by the federal government. Public works, he felt, should be subsidized by the states, just as New York had done in building the Erie Canal. After all, he argued, if New York could finance public improvements, so, too, could all other states.

In addition to reasserting Jefferson's governmental creed, Van Buren hoped to bring about the "substantial reorganization" of Jefferson's old party, to unite the North and the South, to forge an alliance between what he termed the planters of the South and the plain people of the North, to form what would become the Democratic party. Such a "reorganization" would furnish, he wrote, "a complete antidote for sectional prejudices"; moreover, it would quiet the "clamour [against] Southern Influence and African Slavery."

So, in the winter of 1826-1827, in order to reorganize Jefferson's old party and, naturally, to support Jackson's election to the presidency against the incumbent, John Quincy Adams, Van Buren initiated several alliances with politicians from other sections of the country.

There were a number of men involved, many of them Congressmen. The most prominent included Thomas Hart Benton, Senator from Missouri; Thomas Ritchie, editor of the Richmond *Enquirer* and the head of the Richmond Junto, Virginia's equivalent of the Albany Regency; and, perhaps most important of all, John C. Calhoun of South Carolina.

Calhoun was the first man Van Buren spoke to about reorganizing the party. They met late in December 1826 at the home of William H. Fitzhugh in Georgetown, right outside Washington. Van Buren sat leisurely in an oversized chair, one leg dangling over the other, calmly reviewing the need for structuring a reinvigorated party around Jackson so that his election would really mean something. In passing, Van Buren ventured that such a condition would diminish sectional tensions over slavery. For Calhoun, this was a telling point.

As the little man continued speaking Calhoun peered intently at him, his nimble brain catching all the subtle nuances of the New Yorker's arguments. A Jackson victory, Van Buren concluded, "as the result of his military services without reference to party . . . would be one thing. His election as the result of a combined and concerted effort of a political party, holding, in the main, to certain tenets and opposed to certain prevailing principles, might be another and far different thing."

Calhoun was extremely impressed by Van Buren's suggestions, particularly since it was understood that he would be Jackson's vice-presidential running mate. Finally, he rose from his chair and as a gesture of consent stretched out his hand, which Van Buren quickly grasped. From this simple beginning, from this alliance between a planter of the South and one of the "plain people" of the North, the Democratic party eventually emerged. True, the two men could not speak for the majority of voters of the North and the South, but they had tremendous influence among many politicians from their respective sections, and their advice and arguments would be given great weight. In time Calhoun would come to represent the special interests of the South. He became the defender and pleader for what he called the South's "peculiar institution"—slavery. It is interesting therefore that now, in 1826, in arguing the merits of a revitalized alliance between North and South, Van Buren should mention the cessation of Northern criticism of "African slavery" as an important consequence.

Like Van Buren, John C. Calhoun had been born in 1782—March 18th, to be exact. But there the similarity ends. That Calhoun and the Little Magician came from very different sections of the country was extremely meaningful in the long run. He was born in the South Carolina uplands near the Savannah River. Educated at Yale College, he studied law at Tapping Reeve's school at Litchfield, Connecticut, and was admitted to the South Carolina bar. He began his political career with a speech in 1807 at a public meeting in which he denounced Britain's aggressions against American maritime rights. He was elected to the South Carolina legislature and then to the U.S. House of Representatives.

Calhoun's appearance in Congress in 1810, along with Henry Clay of Kentucky, Felix Grundy of Tennessee, and Peter B. Porter of New York, brought together a group of Congressmen who were highly nationalistic and intensely anti-British. For the wrongs committed by England against the United States since the Revolution, such as the impressment of American seamen and the seizure of American ships on the high seas, these young Congressmen urged the country to declare war and thereby redress these terrible indignities to the nation's honor. Because of their belligerency they were called "War Hawks." By their oratorical and organizational skills they eventually succeeded in prodding the Congress into a declaration of war.

Shortly after the War of 1812, James Monroe won election as President of the United States and named Calhoun his Secretary of War. And a right fine Secretary he was, too. Efficient, intelligent, and imaginative, he used his talents and position to strengthen national defense. He was the administration's most nationalistic spokesman, arguing, pleading, cajoling Congress for funds to improve the country's defenses.

But by the 1820s Calhoun's intense nationalistic feeling for the country as a whole began to wane. He became convinced that the Northern section of the nation was taking advantage of the Southern section, particularly with respect to the tariff—the tax on foreign imports. The increased industrialization of the North after the War of 1812 brought steady demands from manufacturers for tariff protection of their products from foreign competition. Northerners wanted foreign goods taxed to jack up their prices, so that lower-priced domestic products could enjoy a wider market at home. Southerners argued that such tariffs were unfair. They sold their staple crop, cotton, on a world market in which the price was determined by the laws of supply and demand but were forced to buy manufactured products at home on a closed market protected by tariff laws. To Southerners, therefore, tariffs, enacted by

43

Congress, were nothing more than a government subsidy paid to Northern manufacturers out of the pockets of Southern planters and farmers.

Quickly responding to the temper of his constituents, to the needs of his section of the country, Calhoun denounced Congressional efforts to raise tariff rates. Also, cotton prices had been declining steadily for the past few years, and he blamed this slide on the tariff rates enacted by Congress in 1824. And as the price of cotton continued to fall, Calhoun's youthful ideals about a strong central government and federally financed fortifications and public works fell with it. By 1826 he was no longer an ardent nationalist but rather a sectionalist, a man devoted to the needs and problems of his own section, the South. With enormous energy and intellectual power he set about defending the rights of the states.

As he grew older, Calhoun became more and more the theoretician, more and more the advocate of states' rights. His disposition grew sour as he contemplated the future of South Carolina, the South, and its "peculiar institution," slavery. To some observers he was "the cast-iron man," who looked as though he had never been born; and because of the intensity of his feelings he looked as though he could never be extinguished, never consumed. After the 1828 election, when he became Jackson's Vice-President and presided over the Senate, he would stare fixedly at whoever was speaking, concentrating on every word. Sometimes his dark eyes would flash with anger or disagreement if he sensed danger to his ideas or to the South. When he spoke, it was close, rapid, theoretical. Listeners said it was extremely interesting to hear him talk because there was a never failing evidence of high intellect. But after a while listeners turned away, for Calhoun lost the power to communicate with people. More and more he grew to live in "utter intellectual solitude." When he met friends, he didn't converse with them, he harangued them. And he did it everywhere—in the street, in the Senate, by the fireside. He spoke rapidly in whole paragraphs, pausing briefly to allow his listener a word or two in response. But he either dismissed what had been said to him or twisted it into what he wanted to hear. The pause over, Calhoun would begin his lecture anew.

Yet Calhoun had not achieved political distinction because he turned men away. He was in fact a man of powerful intellect, deep convictions, and political astuteness with strong support from South Carolina and other leaders from the South as well as wide respect throughout the nation.

This handsome, highly romantic portrait shows John C. Calhoun before frustration, resentment and anger etched his face. Contemporaries always noticed the black, flashing eyes.

Which explains why Van Buren had gone to him in 1826 and spoken ardently for a revival of a North-South alliance as the basis of a revitalized party which would elect Jackson in 1828. Calhoun was designated Jackson's vice-presidential running mate and expected to succeed Old Hickory in the White House whenever the General stepped down.

But there was one danger Calhoun did not bring up in his conversation with Van Buren. It went back to 1818, when Jackson had invaded and seized Spanish Florida. Calhoun, who was the Secretary of War at the time, took offense at the action. Not that he cared much about the Spanish or wasn't glad to see Florida eventually annexed by the United States. What bothered him was Jackson's failure to consult him and gain his permission before the invasion. The General had bypassed him. He had gone over Calhoun's head to the President. So miffed was the Secretary that he counseled President Monroe to reprimand Jackson. Monroe rejected this advice, but fortunately for Calhoun did not broadcast it. Otherwise, Jackson, who was extremely sensitive about his military exploits and reputation, would have nailed Calhoun as an enemy and the South Carolinian would never have been designated as the General's vice-presidential running-mate ten years later.

There were rumors of Calhoun's true feelings about the Florida invasion, but nothing substantial—nothing to cause Van Buren to back away from him as a collaborator in restructuring the old Jeffersonian party. In any event, as of 1826 Van Buren and Calhoun agreed to bring their supporters into alliance behind Jackson and to encourage as many other national leaders to join them as possible. Van Buren promised to write his allies in Pennsylvania. In addition, the Little Magician offered to tour the South in the spring of 1827 to assure Southern politicos of Northern goodwill.

In concluding this North-South alliance the collaborators did not forget the West. And aside from Jackson himself, the most important Westerner to be drawn into the combination that finally became the Democratic party was Thomas Hart Benton of Missouri.

Benton was a big, powerful-looking man with an ego twice the size of his physique. He had black, curly hair, side whiskers, and a long nose that wandered crookedly down his face. When he spoke he *sounded* powerful, too powerful to be contradicted. He was a great talker, too—loud, forceful, a bit bombastic at times, but very effective.

Benton was born at Harts Mill, near Hillsboro, North Carolina, on

March 14, 1782—the same year as Van Buren and Calhoun—and attended the University of North Carolina, then called Chapel Hill College, where he studied law. He moved to Tennessee in 1806, was elected to the state senate three years later, and became Jackson's aide-de-camp during the Creek War. Unfortunately, Benton and Jackson fell into a terrible quarrel that ruptured their relations for many years. It began as a dispute over a very obscure point of honor between Jesse Benton, Thomas's brother, and Billy Carroll, a brigade inspector in Jackson's army. It ended with Jackson slumped on a barroom floor, his shoulder shattered by a slug and his left arm pierced by a bullet that buried itself near the bone.

After the gunfight Nashville was no longer a healthy place for the Bentons. Jackson's friends took his wounding as an unkind deed for which they felt they must have adequate satisfaction. "I am literally in hell here," Thomas Hart Benton wrote shortly afterward. He had, he said, "the meanest wretches under heaven to contend with—liars, affidavit-makers, and shameless cowards. All the puppies of Jackson are at work on me; but they will be astonished at what will happen; for it is not them, but their master, whom I will hold accountable. . . . I am in the middle of hell, and see no alternative but to kill or be killed; for I will not crouch to Jackson; and the fact that I and my brother defeated him and his tribe, and broke his small sword in the public square, will for ever rankle in his bosom and make him thirst after vengeance. My life is in danger; nothing but a decisive duel can save me, or even give me a chance for my own existence; for it is a settled plan to turn out puppy after puppy to bully me, and when I have got into a scrape, to have me killed somehow in the scuffle, and afterwards the affidavit-makers will prove it was honorably done."

Benton was a sensible man. He didn't have to wait to be killed to know what he must do. He resigned his commission in the army at the close of the War of 1812 and headed west to Missouri. Benton rose quickly in Missouri politics. When the state was admitted into the Union in 1821, Benton became one of its U.S. Senators. In Congress he soon demonstrated his prowess as a skillful parliamentarian. He knew how to weave and maneuver during Senate debates to get his way. Most important of all, he was an extremely influential Western politician. If Jackson had ambitions for the presidency, and if he were ever elected President, Benton could be a valuable friend. So, since both men became U.S. Senators in the 1820s, it wasn't long before Benton and

Jackson met in Washington. Ten years had passed since their quarrel. Would they lunge at one another? Would they draw pistols? No one was quite sure what would happen. But Jackson, an older man who wanted the presidency and understood Benton's potential usefulness, stepped up to his old enemy and asked him about the health of his wife. Amazed and somewhat pleased, Benton responded quickly and returned the inquiry. That's all that happened. The meeting was as brief as it was unexpected. A few days later Jackson called at Benton's lodgings, and not finding him home left his card. Then, the next time the Missouri Senator saw the General, he bowed. Jackson shot out his hand. The two men shook hands and dissolved their old hatred. In the political wars ahead each found the other a bastion of strength and support.

But poor Jesse, Thomas's brother, never forgot and never forgave. In the presidential election of 1828 he was still trying to injure Jackson. He wrote a pamphlet vilifying the General, attempting to prove he was unfit to sit in the White House. It was especially mortifying for him to know that his own brother had deserted to his enemy. He never forgot that.

But Jesse had one satisfaction. The bullet fired so long ago at Jackson still lodged in the old man's arm, giving him at times considerable discomfort. As the years passed, the bullet flattened itself against the bone and threatened to cause paralysis. Another ten years and the pain was so intense that it was decided the bullet had to be removed. So, with Jackson fully conscious and gritting his teeth, the doctor probed and dug into the arm and finally caught hold of the flattened metal and pulled it out. Jackson was almost unconscious when the operation ended. In jest, someone standing nearby offered the souvenir to Thomas Hart Benton, supposedly the owner of the bullet. The Senator refused, observing that Jackson had acquired legal title to it in common law by twenty years' possession. But it had been only nineteen years.

"Oh, well," said Benton, "in consideration of the extra care he had taken of it—keeping it constantly about his person, and so on—I'll waive the odd year."

It was Benton's tremendous influence among Western Congressmen, as well as his debating and parliamentary talents in the Senate, that led Van Buren to solicit his support in 1827 in the creation of the Democratic party. Benton quickly agreed to the alliance since he could not abide Adams. Besides, it would help him reestablish his friendship with Jackson now that Jackson was this party's presidential candidate. So the alliance between the North and the South was extended to include the West. The Democratic party would be a national party.

The leaders of this revitalized party—and there were dozens more besides Van Buren, Calhoun and Benton—were all first-rate politicians. They were expert organizers. And the organization was structured from top to bottom, from local "Hickory Clubs" in the communities to central corresponding committees in the states that sought to unify the efforts of the Jacksonians on the national (Congressional) level. Hundreds of newspapers were founded. Politicians knew that the press was perhaps the greatest unifying political force as well as very influential in shaping the public mind. With a newspaper, said Van Buren, "we can endure a thousand convulsions. Without it, we might as well hang our harps on the willows."

At one meeting of Jacksonian Congressmen it was agreed that they would sponsor "a chain of newspaper posts, from the New England States to Louisiana, and branching off through Lexington to the Western States." So rapid was this journalistic expansion that it was officially announced in 1828 that there were six hundred newspapers—most of them political—published in the country, fifty of them dailies, a hundred fifty semiweeklies and four hundred weeklies. In the presidential election of 1828 the country was literally wrapped in political paper. The American people were battered with millions of words telling them what they must do and how they must vote to save the Republic.

But it takes money to run a campaign and manage a national party, and costs run high when the communications media are extensively used. So the Democrats developed or improved a wide variety of techniques to raise money to pay political costs. At local meetings and conventions the delegates were usually taxed a fixed amount to meet printing costs. One Ohio county central committee requested each ward "to appoint a fund committee . . . for the purpose of receiving . . . contributions . . . and that the same be paid over to the treasurer of the general committee of the county." Elsewhere, public dinners and banquets were held to defray costs. As usual, large contributions were solicited from those who could afford it or whose interest depended on Democratic goodwill. And frequently, newspaper editors were designated official printers to Congress or to state legislatures to print documents, reports, journals and the like, which brought the newspapers a sizeable subsidy.

Most of the money was used to encourage greater public participation in the elective process. Now that there were so many voters, politicians began devising new schemes and methods to capture the mass electorate. One way they learned to win the electorate was to nominate for office men of wide popular appeal. A Hero, for example, like General Andrew Jackson. Someone attractive. Someone who could excite enthusiasms in the people. Someone who possessed charisma. Another way was to provide an attractive election campaign. So these politicians developed a number of new and flashy schemes to amuse and delight the masses. In the process they recast the style and tone of American politics. As they had initiated the modern political system, they also created the modern political campaign style.

For example, they introduced songs and slogans into election campaigns. They inaugurated parades, barbecues, tree plantings, dinners, rallies. They provided buttons and clothes to designate one's party and candidate; and through a chain of newspapers covering the nation they turned out a mountain of party propaganda, including cartoons, songs, and funny stories. These politicians believed that the public responded to stimulation, so the bigger the stimulus the bigger the response. The Age of Jackson marked the beginning of the kind of electioneering which employed gimmicks of all kinds to arouse and sustain popular interest in the activities of the party.

One of the more effective gimmicks invented by the Democrats was the use of the hickory as a symbol of their candidate and party. Since Jackson was known as Old Hickory it was an easy and obvious symbol. But as the Democratic party began to take organizational shape, hickory sticks, hickory canes, hickory brooms shot up across the country, at crossroads, on steeples, on steamboats, in the hands of children— everywhere. Poles made of hickory were erected "in every village, as well as upon the many city streets." Many of them were standing as late as 1845, rotting mementoes of democracy's advance. Local Democratic clubs and militia companies also organized ceremonies to plant hickory trees in their village and town squares as part of their campaign to heighten public interest in the election.

Barbecues were also popular in stimulating public interest. In Baltimore a "Grand Barbecue" was arranged by the Democrats ostensibly to commemorate the successful defense of the city against British attack during the War of 1812. But it actually became a barbecue for Andrew Jackson. Three bullocks were roasted and each man at the affair was expected to wear a hickory leaf in his hat to show his political preference. The festivities began with the firing of a cannon, followed by a "thrilling" parade of over seven hundred men—"gentlemen of the exchange, blacksmiths, tanners, carpenters, masons, butchers and men from all trades . . . in fact the best part of the bone and sinew of the town was there.'' After the parade someone called for a cheer. But for whom? The brave defenders of the city during the late war? Without a moment's pause, the crowd instinctively cheered for Andrew Jackson.

These scenes of contagious and raucous enthusiasm for Old Hickory—the sort of thing that happened later at Jackson's inauguration—were carefully staged by Democrats. They didn't simply happen. They were made to happen. They were believed to be essential in "creating" popular majorities for Democratic candidates—all the candidates, not Jackson alone. "Van Buren has learned you know that the *Hurra Boys* were for Jackson . . ." wrote one critic, "and to my regret they constitute a powerful host.''

To encourage the *Hurra Boys* and whip up even greater excitement for the General and his party, some politicians toyed with the idea of bringing Jackson himself to their meetings, although that clearly violated tradition and ran the risk of provoking resentment. Presidential candidates were expected to stay home and keep their mouths shut, leaving it to others to solicit votes for their candidacy. So, being a proper and politically cautious man, Jackson refused all invitations to display himself publicly—all, that is, except one. He chose to accept an invitation of the Louisiana Central Committee to attend a ceremony in New Orleans on January 8, 1828, to commemorate his victory over the British in 1815. Ostensibly the celebration was nonpolitical, so Jackson could attend without eliciting a barrage of criticism from those who opposed his election. Even so, the ceremony was arranged and publicized to remind the American people of their "undying gratitude" to the Hero. Representatives from many state Democratic delegations attended, along with the General. As reported in the newspapers, the celebration was "the most stupendous thing of the kind that had ever occurred in the United States." The welcoming ceremony, the speeches, parades, and dinner were unlike anything ever seen before. "The World has never witnessed so glorious, so wonderful a Celebration—" exclaimed a participant, "never has *Gratitude & Patriotism* so happily united, so beautifully blended—& it will form a bright page in American history.''

The delight with which the people responded to this new brand of electioneering encouraged politicians to program a wider assortment of entertainments, including songs, jokes, cartoons, funny stories, poems

51

and puns. The newspapers carried some of the best jokes and funny sayings, most of which poked fun at the incumbent President, John Quincy Adams, and his Secretary of State, Henry Clay.

"Hurrah for Jackson," said one man.

"Hurrah for the Devil," replied another who opposed Jackson's election.

"Very well," retorted the Democrat. "You stick to your candidate and I'll stick to mine."

One story was told of a man who found the friends of Adams like the Frenchman who boasted that King Louis had spoken to him.

"What did the King say to you?" asked an awed friend.

"He told me to get out of his way," replied the delighted Frenchman.

And there were puns. Most of them were pretty ghastly, like the following:

Question: "Why is Adams on ticklish grounds?"
Answer: "Because he stands on slippery Clay."

Sometimes the politicians simply pandered to the worst instincts and tastes of the electorate, but it was all done to awaken interest and concern in politics, to bring people to the polls to register outrage or faith or enthusiasm. And the great number of new voters who exercised their franchise during the Jacksonian era and who flocked to Washington to cheer their approval of Old Hickory upon his inauguration justified all the efforts of professional politicians and did, in fact, link them closer to the operation of government. Seeing these masses, reading the constant rise of the number of voters exercising the ballot, and looking at the candidates elected to office—every one of them, not simply Jackson alone—provided all the proof needed to argue that popular government had indeed arrived in the United States.

4

The National Republican Party

DEMOCRATIZING THE ELECTORAL process was not the accomplishment of the leaders of the Democratic party alone. Other politicians had a hand in bringing the masses into political action. These men opposed the Democratic party and called themselves National Republicans. They were led by such distinguished statesmen as Henry Clay, Daniel Webster, and, to a more limited extent, the incumbent President, John Quincy Adams.

They called themselves National Republicans because of their emphasis on the role of the federal government in directing the nation's economic growth. They reaffirmed the philosophy of Alexander Hamilton, which defined federal power as broadly as possible, and they pursued a series of goals which had originally been formulated by Henry Clay when he was a Congressman from Kentucky.

Fun-loving, hard-drinking, quick to accept a bet, Henry Clay was a hail-fellow, affable, delightful man whom everyone enjoyed and respected. Tall and thin, with great hollows gouged in both cheeks and a thin, almost invisible line marking the location of his mouth, Clay looked like a west-country farmer. But when he spoke, either in public or private, one realized what a remarkable man he was, how keen his political talents, how wide-ranging the thrust of his mind.

Clay was born in Virginia in 1777, clerked in several law offices until he obtained a license, and then moved to Kentucky. He was elected to the U.S. Congress, where his brain and tongue won him an immediate reputation as a persuasive and influential legislator. Although quite young—he was barely 33—he was chosen Speaker of the House of Representatives, and, as leader of the War Hawks faction just prior to the War of 1812, he placed his friends and allies on important committees to better control the operation of the House affairs and win a declaration of war against Great Britain.

After the war he became a leading critic of the Monroe administration, largely because he was denied the cabinet post he wanted. In an effort to embarrass the administration, he led the fight to win Congressional censure of Jackson for the General's invasion of Spanish Florida. Clay denied personal hostility to Jackson or Monroe. In a speech before a packed House of Representatives he said he was simply doing his duty, acting from principle. Other members, he continued, "may bear down all opposition . . . even vote the general the public thanks; they may carry him triumphantly through this House. But, if they do, in my humble judgment, it will be a triumph of the principle of insubordination—a triumph of the military over the liberties of the people."

Quite predictably, when Jackson read this speech, he erupted into a towering passion. Warned beforehand that Congress might censure him for invading foreign soil without authorization, he raced to Washington to defend his actions, which he believed perfectly legal because they had been sanctioned by President Monroe. "The hypocracy [sic] & baseness of Clay . . ." Jackson wrote to a friend, "make me despise the Villain. . . . I hope you will roast him in the West."

That was the beginning of Jackson's long hatred for Henry Clay. And it intensified over the years. In any event, the censure failed and Jackson always remained highly sensitive to any criticism of his Florida campaign.

In a series of speeches Clay delivered before the Senate in 1824, he outlined several proposals—subsequently called the "American System"—which became the fundamental program of the National Republican party. To begin with, Clay urged building public works at federal expense. Federal construction of roads, bridges, highways, canals would help bind together all the great sections of the nation— East, West, North, and South. For example, the farmer in the West

54

could, with improved transportation, more easily ship his produce to the cities in the East. With the money he received from the sale of his produce he could buy the Eastern manufactured goods he needed. Thus, both the Western farmer and the Eastern manufacturer would prosper, and the ties uniting the nation would be strengthened.

To encourage American industry, Clay proposed a protective tariff so that manufacturers could withstand the fearful competition of foreign goods, particularly British goods, when, after the War of 1812, Britain began dumping her products on the American market. Also, Clay favored a sound banking system supported by the federal government, with stable currency and ready credit which could expand and contract according to the needs of business. He therefore strongly favored continuing the Second National Bank, chartered in 1816, which was operating very efficiently under the able direction of its president, Nicholas Biddle.

Clay claimed his American system—internal improvements, tariff protection, sound currency, and credit—would benefit all geographical sections and economic classes of the country and quickly establish the nation in the front ranks of modern industrial societies. But his program required direct governmental action; it meant strengthening the central government and enlarging its powers to direct and influence the financial affairs of the American people. Those who saw advantage and merit in the American System gravitated to the National Republican party. Those who worried about enlarging the power of the federal government entered the Democratic party.

There was another side—a noneconomic side—to the principles and program of the National Republicans. That side was largely the contribution of John Quincy Adams, running for reelection against Jackson in 1828. He believed the federal government should be responsible for the nation's intellectual and cultural progress. He advocated founding a national university, since knowledge, he said, was the first instrument for the betterment of man. In addition, he proposed building an astronomical observatory to study the phenomena of the heavens. In Europe there were upward of 130 such "light-houses of the skies," he wrote, while in America there was not one. Moreover, he urged systematic and scientific exploration of both the western territories and the entire northeastern coastline to discover and publicize the resources and capabilities of the American continent. Adams also proposed establishing a naval academy similar to West Point (this was achieved much later by a Democratic administration), a Department of the In-

The set mouth, gaunt expression and sharp angles of Henry Clay's face are softened somewhat in this idealized portrait. It does show, however, his commanding presence and self-confidence.

terior, a more effective patent law to protect inventors, and an improved and uniform standard of weights and measures to replace the hodgepodge currently (and still) practiced.

Unquestionably, Adams was an intellectual giant. Unfortunately, he was also a political pigmy. Short and balding, he looked as dour and forbidding as the most stereotyped of colonial Puritans. "I am a man of reserved, cold, austere and forbidding manners," he frankly admitted in his diary. "My political adversaries say, a gloomy misanthrope; and my personal enemies an unsocial savage. With a knowledge of the actual defects in my character, I have not the pliability to reform it."

Son of John Adams, the revolutionary patriot and second President, John Quincy Adams was raised to become President of the United States. He was expected to be a great man, and it placed a terrible burden on him all the days of his life. His mother, the extraordinarily intelligent and strong-willed Abigail Smith Adams, took him to Bunker Hill as a young boy to see the site of the famous engagement between American patriots and British soldiers so that he would understand the obligations and sacrifices the cause of liberty and freedom entailed. She had him read ancient history day after day because she felt it was the best way to inspire him with a sense of public duty as well as teach him the lessons of statesmanship. To further his education he was sent to Russia at the age of fourteen to serve as private secretary to Francis Dana, who had been sent by Congress as minister to the court of Catherine the Great. After fourteen months, young Adams journeyed to Paris, where he served as his father's secretary until 1785. The elder Adams, at the time, was United States minister to France. Between mother and father, John Quincy Adams had been programed for the highest public service, and they expected him to fulfill their ambitions for him. In repeated letters to his mother he assured her he wanted to be a "good boy" and become the man she desired.

Returning to the United States, Adams attended Harvard College, studied law, and in 1791 was appointed minister to the Netherlands by President George Washington. Later he headed the missions to Portugal, Prussia, and Russia and served as one of five commissioners who negotiated the peace treaty with Great Britain that ended the War of 1812. Appointed Secretary of State by President James Monroe in 1817, Adams climaxed a successful diplomatic career by becoming a brilliant Secretary, probably the greatest Secretary of State in American history. With Jackson's military help, Adams won the diplomatic battles to

57

This late daguerreotype, taken a year before John Quincy Adams's death, documents everything ever said about him as a brooding, sour-faced misanthrope.

acquire Florida and established a strong American presence in the far northwest, thus transforming the United States into a continental power. He was also the principal architect of the Monroe Doctrine.

In 1824 Adams had run for the presidency. Because there were many other candidates, including Jackson, Clay, and William H. Crawford, no one received a majority of electoral votes. And so, following the requirements of the Twelfth Amendment to the Constitution, the election was thrown for decision to the House of Representatives. On the first ballot the House chose Adams the sixth President of the United States, fulfilling the dream of his aged father and late mother.

Adam's first act as President was to choose Henry Clay to be his Secretary of State. The announcement of this appointment horrified the Jacksonians. "Corrupt bargain!" they raged. Before the House election, they claimed, Clay had obviously offered to throw his support to Adams in return for the secretaryship because that post usually led immediately to the presidency. At least it had for the last twenty years. In the Senate, John Randolph of Roanoke roasted both Adams and Clay in a wild speech full of Latin quotations, literary allusions, European history, and practically everything else the Virginia Senator carried in his intellectual baggage. "Let Judas have his thirty pieces of silver," he roared. This way they could buy "a Potter's field in which to inter this miserable Constitution of ours, crucified between two gentlemen." He ended his speech with a shocker, including a wild analogy to the novel *Tom Jones.* "I was defeated, horse, foot, and dragoons—cut up—and clean broke down—by the coalition of Blifil and Black George—by the combination, unheard of till then, of the Puritan and the black-leg."

Black-leg! Now it was Clay's turn to rage. Immediately he challenged Randolph to a duel. Randolph accepted with an announcement that he had no intention of making Mrs. Clay a widow. On April 6, 1826, the two hotheads met across the Potomac River from Georgetown near a place called Little Falls Bridge. It was late in the afternoon. The weapons: pistols. The distance: ten paces.

As the two men took their places the sun was just beginning to set behind the Virginia hills. On signal by the second, both men fired. Both fortunately missed. Randolph's bullet struck the stump behind Clay, and Clay's bullet kicked up the dirt behind Randolph. Thomas Hart Benton, who had been trying to prevent the duel and had come along as a witness, now tried to stop the fight. But Clay waved him aside. "This is child's play," he sneered.

Benton then asked Randolph to disengage but was again refused. So the seconds reloaded the pistols. Again the signal was given and again two shots rang out. Clay aimed to kill but the eccentric Randolph raised his arm high and fired into the air. As he did so, he said, "I do not fire at you, Mr. Clay."

There was a pause. Then Randolph walked toward his adversary and extended his hand, which Clay clasped with great vigor. In a voice half choked with emotion, Clay exclaimed, "I trust in God, my dear sir, you are untouched: after what has occurred I would not have harmed you for a thousand worlds."

Randolph looked down at his coat. Clay's second shot had torn a hole through it and come dangerously close to Randolph's hip. Laughing, almost like a maniac, the Virginian said, "You owe me a coat, Mr. Clay."

So ended this ridiculous duel. But it silenced neither Randolph nor the Jacksonians. In the presidential campaign two years later in which Adams ran for reelection, the issue raised most often by the Jacksonians was the so-called "corrupt bargain" charge. And the more Clay protested his innocence the more he convinced people of his guilt.

Clay tried desperately to help Adams defeat Jackson in 1828, but it was a losing propositon almost from the very beginning. The election was reduced to two candidates and so the possibility of final selection again falling to the House of Representatives seemed very remote. And with Jackson's great popularity, the managerial skill of the Democrats, and the burning issue of "corrupt bargain," the outcome seemed a foregone conclusion. Still Clay kept up a good running battle for Adams, refusing to believe that the American people would prefer a "military chieftain" over a President and statesman of proven talent in the tradition of Washington, Jefferson, and Madison. Employing every political device he knew to be effective, Clay prepared to purge the government of all officeholders who opposed the Adams administration. "Henceforth," he wrote one friend, "I think the principle ought to be steadily adhered to of appointing only friends to the Administration in public offices. Such I believe is the general conviction in the Cabinet." But President Adams publicly denounced any attempt to use patronage—rewards of public office—to influence politics. He solemnly promised to appoint men whom he believed worthy of office, irrespective of party. But he later admitted he was "importuned to serve my friends and reproached for neglecting them, because I will not dismiss, or drop from Executive offices, able and faithful political opponents to provide for my own partisans.''

Such noble sentiments only made Clay's job more difficult. Patronage is the very lifeblood of political parties, unless there are large financial contributors who are willing to subsidize the tremendous costs of campaigning. And parties financed by wealth function for wealth. So, in a sense, patronage distribution was a splendid means of preventing political control by the rich. Those who worked for a successful candidate could expect a reward once he took office. Realistic politicians like Clay understood this. Not so John Quincy Adams.

Fortunately, Clay was not alone in his efforts to reelect Adams in 1828. He had the considerable assistance of a number of stalwarts, the most important of whom was Daniel Webster of Massachusetts. Between them they constructed a firm base on which to erect their new National Republican party.

Daniel Webster had a strange career. Like Calhoun he started out by going in one political direction and ended up going another. Where Calhoun began as a nationalist and slowly evolved into a states' righter and finally a secessionist, Webster started as an advocate of the states and their rights and then shifted to a strong nationalistic position.

''Black Dan,'' they had called him as a boy. At a tavern one day in Concord, General John Stark, who had fought at the Battle of Bennington during the Revolution, peered at the young Daniel Webster and then with all the candor of age fortified by several stiff drinks said: ''Daniel, your face is pretty black, but it isn't so black as your father's was with gunpowder at the Bennington fight.''

True, Daniel Webster was quite dark, so swarthy in fact that some people jokingly told him he looked like an Indian. But when he opened his mouth and started to speak he made sounds such as no Indian—or anyone else for that matter—could imitate. It was a big voice, a bit higher-pitched than one might expect, but rich-sounding and very compelling. By 1825, he was the greatest speaker in New England, and was invited to give an address at the laying of the cornerstone for a monument on Bunker Hill to commemorate the fiftieth anniversary of the famous battle. A great crowd, including General Lafayette, who was then touring in the United States, turned out to hear ''Black Dan.''

As Webster rose to speak, the crowd, estimated at ten thousand, hushed to hear every word. He began slowly, reviewing for his audience the many changes that had taken place during the last half century,

61

The hypnotic stare, bushy eyebrows, bulging forehead, combined with a monumental voice and magnificent delivery, made the "Godlike" Daniel Webster America's greatest orator.

describing how the country had prospered and how the people had advanced under a free government. At one point he turned to the small group of surviving veterans of the Bunker Hill battle and addressed himself directly to them. "Venerable Men," he began. Then he stopped and looked at the few old men seated in the place of honor. "But alas! you are not all here," he continued. "Time and the sword have thinned your ranks."

Having paid due respect to the past, Webster turned to the future, which was the real theme of his speech. The fate of popular government, he said, depends on the success of the political experiment in the United States. "The last hopes of mankind, therefore, rest with us"—with the Union. "Let us cultivate a true spirit of union and harmony. Let us act under a settled conviction, and an habitual feeling, that these twenty-four States are one country." But this nationalistic position was relatively new for Webster, for he had started political life as an intense advocate of states' rights.

Webster had been brought up in New Hampshire, where he was born in 1782—the same year as Van Buren, Calhoun, and Benton. (It was a remarkable year—1782!) Educated at Dartmouth College, he became a lawyer and was elected to Congress from New Hampshire on a platform that condemned the War of 1812—called "Mr. Madison's War" by many New Englanders—and even hinted at secession. The merchants and shipowners of New England had been making money trading with Britain, and the war jeopardized their profits. In a public letter addressed to President Madison, Webster wrote: "We shrink from the separation of the states as an event fraught with incalculable evils." But if it comes, he continued, the fault will rest with the administration and its fire-eating friends from the South and West. Supported by shipping and mercantile interests who were staunchly hostile to the administration and the war, Webster had no difficulty winning election to Congress for several terms.

After the war, when men like Clay and Calhoun were publicly arguing for a strong national government, Webster defended the states and their rights. Like his constituents, he insisted that the national government possessed only limited powers. He emphatically opposed federally sponsored internal improvements, protective tariffs and a national bank.

In 1816 Webster moved from New Hampshire to Boston because he felt Massachusetts held many more opportunities for a rising lawyer and politician. Indeed, almost overnight, his career shot forward. Soon he was arguing cases before the United States Supreme Court. After his successful performance before this court in the Dartmouth College case, he was hired to argue *McCulloch* vs. *Maryland* and *Gibbons* vs. *Ogden.* All these decisions were historic. Many of them, as announced by Chief Justice John Marshall, were culled directly from Webster's arguments.

Webster's success in the courts, usually in defense of business interests in Massachusetts, rapidly advanced his political career. Besides allowing him to buy stock in their corporations and paying him substantial legal fees, Massachusetts businessmen supported his bid for election to Congress starting in 1823, first as Representative and then as Senator. And his unique speaking and legal talents promptly vaulted him to the front ranks of Congressional leadership.

But where initially New England had had heavy investments in shipping and mercantile interests and had objected to the tariff—along with all the other features of Clay's American System—now, in the period following the War of 1812, New England had turned to industry and had begun shifting her capital from shipping to manufactures. Consequently, protecting northeastern manufactures from lower-priced foreign goods by means of a tariff seemed a matter of necessity. In time Henry Clay's entire American System became exceedingly attractive to New England—internal improvements, bank, tariff, everything.

As the interests and needs of his constituents slowly changed, so too did Webster's ideas about the role of government in aiding the economic well-being of the nation. Soon he had changed his position and was arguing for the tariff, at least on those commodities that competed with New England manufactures. Soon he was advocating the merits of the national bank. Indeed, he accepted a retainer's fee from the bank to argue its interests in and out of Congress. Soon he was a full-fledged defender of Clay's entire American System. And, most particularly, he became an ardent nationalist. Gone were his ideas about states' rights. His speeches more and more proclaimed the indissoluble bond between liberty and union. His position stood in stark contrast to the states' rights and secessionist ideas of John C. Calhoun.

Webster had given John Quincy Adams his support in the 1824-25 House presidential election, and he had joined very enthusiastically with Clay to create the National Republican party to try to reelect Adams in 1828. One of the first actions taken by Webster and Clay was to begin a search for that essential ingredient of party building: money. "It seems to me," Clay advised Webster, "that our friends who have the ability should contribute a fund for the purpose of aiding the cause."

Webster was an excellent fund raiser—after all, he had many well-heeled friends—and most of the money either went to Clay himself for dispersal or was distributed as Clay directed. Much of the money went to newspapers to buy support. "The course adopted by the Opposition, in the dissemination of Newspapers and publications against the Administration and supporting presses," declared Clay, "leaves to its friends no other alternative than that of following their example, so far at least as to circulate information among the people." Like the Democrats, Clay and Webster understood the need of influencing the people and persuading them to vote the National Republican ticket.

Clay and Webster also exhorted their friends around the country to organize themselves by forming local committees and holding state conventions. Webster toured New England to ensure its loyalty to Adams and later accepted speaking engagements in Pennsylvania and New York to influence those crucial states. He constantly urged his supporters to "*bestir* themselves" and "rally friends."

And Clay was no less active. "It is a part of the system of the friends of General Jackson," he wrote one partisan, "to make demonstrations—speak boldly—claim every body and every State, and carry the election by storm. The circumstance most to be deprecated is that this system has too much success in dispiriting our friends. You ask my opinion as to the project of a convention in Virginia to nominate, in January next, electors for Mr. Adams. It appears to me to be an excellent project, and one that can not fail to have a good effect."

The National Republicans did indeed hold state conventions, and local rallies and county meetings too. "Political meetings are continually taking place in the different Towns of the State [New Jersey]," explained one National Republican, "where Resolutions are passed and Delegates appointed to attend at Trenton to fix on the Electoral Ticket." At these conventions, central committees and correspondence committees were appointed to keep in communication with similar committees in other states. These interacting committees gave the National Republicans the semblance of a national political organization.

Unfortunately these efforts were woefully uneven throughout the country. The National Republican party was almost nonexistent in the South because of its tariff stance, and in the West the Adams supporters

65

were exceedingly slow in setting up party machinery, resulting occasionally in no machinery at all. Although Clay was admired in most of the West—he was sometimes called "Harry of the West"—it was Jackson who had captured Western affection. Adams as a candidate, on the other hand, was a distinct liability—colorless, drab, unexciting. According to one Western National Republican, the Democrats were "an organized corps, active and well disciplined"; as for his own party, he said, "we have a great many well wishers . . . but no organization."

It was in New England and the middle states of New Jersey, New York, Pennsylvania, Delaware, and Maryland that the National Republicans were strong. The newspapers were particularly effective in chewing over the details of Jackson's "two" marriage ceremonies. Some editors were indignant. "Ought a convicted adultress," wrote one of them of Rachel, "and her paramour husband to be placed in the highest offices of this free and christian land?" Some stories appearing in newspapers came right out of the gutter and were the inventions of desperate editors. "General Jackson's mother was a COMMON PROSTITUTE," read one such item, "brought to this country by the British soldiers! She afterward married a MULATTO MAN, with whom she had several children, of which number General Jackson IS ONE!!!" Old Hickory's reputation as a duelist and gunfighter was also given considerable newspaper coverage. He was maligned as a bully and ruffian, a street brawler, cockfighter, and gambler.

The intensity and scurrility of the propaganda during the 1828 presidential election undoubtedly resulted because both national parties were trying to adjust to the circumstances of a changing society and the vast numbers of new voters they were attempting to control and manage. The Democrats' overwhelming success in winning Jackson's election to the presidency set an example and encouraged both parties to even greater managerial feats in future elections.

But the significance, finally, in the development of party structure and technique was that it got the mass of American voters to participate in the process of selecting the people who run the government. However much Democrats and National Republicans debased the art of debating issues and presenting candidates for office to the electorate, they did bring the people and the government closer together. And that was one of the most lasting and important contributions of the Jacksonian age.

BOOK II
ISSUES AND ANSWERS

(overleaf) The great issues of the day—slavery, union, the Bank, presidential power—were argued and debated in Congress before packed galleries. In this painting, *The Reply to Hayne*, Webster delivers his famous anti-nullification speech, while Calhoun, perched in the presiding officer's chair (in the shadow, left), listens intently.

5

Who Shall Hold Office?

THE ADMINISTRATION OF Andrew Jackson lasted two terms. It stretched from his inauguration on March 4, 1829, until Martin Van Buren, his hand-picked successor, replaced him on March 4, 1837. But to a very large extent the entire fifty-year period between the War of 1812 and the Civil War was the Age of Jackson. And all the experiments in democracy, the alterations of the political process, the extensions of the franchise, the attacks on privilege and deference, the swelling spirit of popular rule—all these were summed up in the phrase "Jacksonian Democracy." It was as though the United States had formed a circle around Jackson to receive the signals and impulses he radiated. Indeed, many of the political vibrations that rocked and jolted the nation during the first half of the nineteenth century resulted directly from his actions and decisions.

Jackson's dynamic force was felt even before he became President— the Florida invasion was only one example—and it would continue to be felt after he left the White House. But the really significant phase of his life, the period in which he had the greatest impact, transpired during the Hero's actual presidency. For his administration grappled with several issues which in their resolution had a profound influence on the course of American life and institutions. These issues included involving more people in the actual running of the government through the rotation system; the problem of holding the Union together; the problem of the Indians; and the struggle for power between the President and the Congress, which resulted in a restructured government.

The first issue was simple and direct: Who shall hold government office? When the masses of people converged on the capital to witness Jackson's inauguration, a large corps of Democratic party newspapermen also streamed into the city to claim their rewards for a contest well fought. They knew they had been valuable to both party and candidate as publicists of the cause, and they were present to receive their just recognition—jobs. From New Hampshire came the brilliant Isaac Hill, a short, lame and cadaverous-looking man who edited the *Patriot* and had helped organize a strong and effective party for Jackson in his state. It was said at the time that he was "determined to revolutionize [New Hampshire] before the end of 1828"—and he practically succeeded. From Kentucky came the wizened, prematurely gray but much talented Amos Kendall, editor of the *Argus of Western America*, who had labored so successfully to unite several party factions in Kentucky behind Jackson to steal that state right out from under Henry Clay's nose.

Other politically important editors who arrived in Washington to share the electoral victory included scholarly Nathaniel Greene, editor of the Boston *Statesman*; quiet Gideon Welles of the New Haven *Journal*; jovial Mordecai M. Noah, editor of the New York City *National Advocate*; energetic Dabney S. Carr of the Baltimore *Republican*; and "from everywhere else," fumed Daniel Webster, "somebody else." It was a large contingent of journalistic and political talent that had come to Washington to "assist Jackson in the establishment of popular rule." Soon these men were meeting daily at the house of Reverend Obadiah B. Brown, a friendly, affable man who doubled as clerk in the Post Office Department during the week and as a minister in the Baptist church on Sundays. Together, they prepared their suggestions and projects for the President to inaugurate "the people's government."

When the group stood outside the east portico of the Capitol on inauguration day and heard Jackson talk about reforming the government by removing the "unfaithful and incompetent," every one of them must have quivered with joy and anticipation. The "rascals" would be thrown out and they, the friends of the masses, would share the rewards, the "spoils" of victory. And true enough, one way or another, either directly or indirectly, they were handsomely repaid. A few of them even exerted a powerful influence on the Jackson administration.

The most powerful was Kendall. Jackson appointed him Fourth Auditor of the Treasury, and from this position he cleared out many of the friends of Adams and Clay and replaced them with certified Democrats. Later he was named Postmaster General, at which time Jackson elevated that post to cabinet level. Henceforth the Postmaster General would control an enormous amount of the federal patronage, and from this position he could pay political debts.

Kendall was also instrumental in winning the President's approval for establishing a new journal in Washington to serve as the official mouthpiece of the Democratic party. As editor, Francis P. Blair was brought in, a mousy-looking man, hardly weighing more than a hundred pounds, who had been Kendall's newspaper associate in Kentucky. On December 7, 1830, the Washington *Globe* began publication, and immediately won national recognition as the voice and mind of the Democratic party, officially approved by Jackson and the leaders of the party in Congress. Blair was a superb editor whose slashing style of writing thoroughly pleased the President.

Isaac Hill, another rough-and-tough-talking editor, was named Second Comptroller of the Treasury. In this office he expected to imitate the style of Kendall in distributing jobs. But he didn't get far, for the Senate refused to confirm his appointment, whereupon he returned to New Hampshire and won election to the United States Senate. As he strolled around the Senate floor he savored every moment of his revenge.

Kendall, Blair, Hill, and several other men became part of a group subsequently known as the "Kitchen Cabinet." This group of unofficial advisers to the President supposedly came to visit Jackson by way of the back stairs through the kitchen. However they got to the President, they successfully claimed his attention and influenced his actions because their ideas almost always mirrored his own. They were all professionals in party politics and they understood how men were managed or manipulated, rewarded or punished to implement the operation of government.

On one particular matter these men were absolutely agreed: the need to "reform" the government by a change of personnel. For these journalists it was a matter of practical politics, the reward for services

Washington seen from across the Potomac seems quiet and rural, yet during this era it was the setting for spectacular Congressional brawls that changed the fate of the nation.

rendered. But for Jackson it was a matter of principle, a matter of democratizing the operation of government. What he wanted understood was that the pervasive notion, traditionally followed up to this time, that government service was the right of the elite—the well educated or the upper class—would no longer be valid under his administration. Jackson believed that government jobs should be open to all. The masses—educated or not, wealthy or not, wellborn or born in obscurity—might not only vote, but hold office as well. Moreover, he contended that it was important in a republic that there be a regular turnover of personnel in government; otherwise office holders become inefficient and corrupt. In time, said Jackson, a bureaucracy emerges which is totally divorced from the people.

His administration would be based on what he called "the principal of rotation." And he proudly proclaimed it to the entire nation in his first annual message to Congress, delivered in December 1829, less than a year after taking office. He flatly stated that the "duties of all public officers are . . . so plain and simple that men of intelligence may readily qualify themselves for their performance. . . . In a country where offices are created solely for the benefit of the people no one man has any more intrinsic right to official station than another." Offices were not established, he continued, to give support to "particular men" at the public expense. No wrong is therefore done by removing them from office, "since neither appointment to nor continuance in office is a matter of right."

To Jackson the principle of rotation directly addressed the problem of how and by whom the government should be run. Jackson believed that through rotation the federal government in Washington could be made to respond directly to the changing demands of the American people as expressed by their ballots. Thus, each new administration, elected by the people, should bring in its own corps of supporters to make certain the policies of that administration were honestly and fairly implemented. Most important, rotation meant that a great many more people would get an opportunity to serve the government. The more people actively involved in the affairs of the nation, the more democratic the system, and the more the problems of the nation get to be widely known and understood. It was an old Jeffersonian principle: Greater participation by the electorate in government safeguards the nation from arbitrary and dictatorial rule. Rotation comes closest to the ideal of making government and its problems available to the largest number of people. But though it was an old principle, Jackson's way of hammering at its importance was new and seemed revolutionary at the time.

Rotation also strengthens the party—the best bulwark of democracy—by placing in the hands of politicians the distribution of jobs (patronage) as rewards, and this nurtures the party organization. But there are dangers: Rotation can be an easy excuse and justification for political head chopping, for regarding government jobs as "spoils" won in a war in which enemies are punished and friends rewarded. When this is the attitude, the best, most efficient, and most dedicated public servants will frequently be removed to make room for party workers whose only interest in office is the money or power involved. When rotation is administered by incompetents or thieves, then everyone suffers and the democratic system is dangerously compromised.

For some politicians, of course, "spoils" is all rotation really means. But to the politician devoted to public service it doesn't mean that at all. Van Buren provides a good example of a politician who used patronage intelligently and with a view to its salutary impact on the operation of government. In New York State he had built his political organization, the Albany Regency, on the skillful use of patronage. In the process he encouraged the careers of such distinguished men as William L. Marcy, Silas Wright, Jr., Benjamin F. Butler, and John A. Dix. But Van Buren ignored the claims of stupid or dishonest politicians and recognized only those men whose intelligence, integrity, ability, and loyalty were outstanding. His machine, as a consequence, was rarely operated by political hacks.

Not that it was simple or easy to dispense patronage with intelligence and skill. Men like Van Buren were hounded for jobs, and it was frequently impossible to shake loose a determined office seeker. Shortly after Jackson's election, Van Buren was designated Secretary of State. In no time the Little Magician was deluged by office seekers. He happened to be in New York City staying at the City Hotel. One young man went looking for him and found the bar in the City Hotel crowded with politicians who had come to "pay their respects" to the Secretary-designate. After a while the doors of the dining room were thrown open and a clerk came in, mounted a chair, and called out:

"Gentlemen who desire to see Mr. Van Buren will please walk into the dining-room."

"We thundered in—" reported the young man, "fifty or sixty of us;

politicians in and out of place; those wanting to get in, those to stay in. We were all hail fellows well met, and there was a roar of jovial talk and banter. Politicians, you know, are friendly to every body; for no man knows who can or who can not forward his views, nor how soon a man now powerless may be in a position to help.''

After a while a waiter entered the room and said, ''Gentlemen, Mr. Van Buren requests your cards.''

Everybody broke out laughing. There was a general fumbling in pockets.

''Cards?'' said the young man. ''What does he want cards for? I have no card with me. I shall write a note.''

While the other office seekers kidded him about his naïveté, the young man scribbled a note which said: ''Sir, I am the bearer of two letters of introduction to you: one from my uncle, Mr. — —, and the other from my friend, the Hon. — —.''

The young man folded his note and placed it on the tray with the cards. The waiter took the tray and withdrew. After a time he returned and solemnly announced:

''Gentlemen, Mr. Van Buren sends his compliments and says he is fatigued with his journey, and requests the honor of your company this evening at eight o'clock, one and all.''

As everyone started to leave, the waiter called to the young man and asked him to wait. Suddenly he became the lion of the room.

''You are a made man,'' said one. ''You'll get the best office in the gift of the government. Not a doubt of it.''

The crowd slowly dispersed. The young man sat some minutes wondering how long he would have to wait and what he would say when he met the great man. ''Without having heard any one enter, I looked up at length, and lo! there, on the opposite side of the fire-place sat the Magician!''

The Little Magician, the Red Fox of Kinderhook, the master builder of the Democratic party! The young man approached his quarry; there was a shaking of hands; the letters were presented and Van Buren read them carefully as though studying each word. After a moment or two Van Buren refolded the letters and said in a voice that was reassuring and almost seductive: ''I highly esteem your uncle, and also your friend. No men in the State stand higher in my regard than they. If I can do anything to oblige them or forward your views, it will give me great pleasure.''

What suavity! what style! thought the young man. A hack politician would have blurted out something like "What can I do for you?" or "As soon as I have something I'll get in touch with you," or "Tell your uncle I'll keep you in mind" or some such. Not Van Buren. Although he knew what the young man was about, he spoke with a subtlety that respected the sensibilities both of himself and the office seeker.

Not unexpectedly, the young man became a clerk in the State Department. He enjoyed a long tenure though he saw many men come and go. Each time there was a new Secretary of State, he did not know for days, sometimes weeks, whether he would be retained. Yet he lasted eight years. Then one morning shortly after a new administration had begun, "a gentleman entered my office, and, presenting his commission, informed me, with the utmost politeness, that I was no longer in the service of the government, and that I saw before me that dread being—terror of all office-holders—A SUCCESSOR!

"I have seen many heads taken off in my time,"he said, "but never one quite so neatly as my own."

When Van Buren arrived in Washington early in 1829 to take up his post as Secretary of State, there was another horde of office seekers waiting for him at his hotel. Even though it was after dark they spotted his coach, surrounded it, and pursued him to his room, where he flopped on a sofa to recover from the tedious journey. Soon the room was filled with people jammed together from wall to wall, and for the next hour they pressed their demands upon him, finally leaving when Van Buren informed them he must go to pay his respects to the President.

Jackson was not better off. In fact his situation was worse. Applicants came right to the White House door and demanded to see "their" President. They were taken directly to him to plead their need. Since this was the "People's government," the people felt no constraint about going directly to the top man and informing him of their wishes. Jackson was so inundated with demands for jobs that he wrote there were five hundred applicants for every office available. Nevertheless he said he was "determined to hear with caution, examine well, and grant offices to none but such as was honest and capable."

Thus, in the early years of the Jackson administration, there appeared to be a mad scramble for office, with politicians of all stripes and talents competing for every favor imaginable. Jackson's enemies circulated stories that during the first year of the "People's government" some two thousand government workers were removed. To men in office from the preceding administration, it seemed like a Democratic "Reign of Terror." There was no other way to describe it. Said one: "Terror . . .

77

reigned in Washington. . . . The great body of officials awaited their fate in silent horror, glad when the office hours expired at having escaped another day.'' There were reports that one man "cut his throat from ear to ear, from the mere terror of being dismissed" while another "has gone raving distracted."

The suspicion and fear of a thoroughgoing purge were aggravated by some Democrats themselves. One of Van Buren's lieutenants in the United States Senate, William L. Marcy, a man of integrity and ability, told his colleagues in the Senate flat out that the removals were justified. "To the victor belong the spoils of the enemy," he baldly asserted, leaving himself open to much misinterpretation. The statement seemed to prove everything Jackson's enemies contended about the removals.

In New York City a man of considerably less integrity, one Samuel Swartwout, described the principle of spoils in very direct and simple terms precisely as he understood it. Unfortunately his letter, later published to the dismay of Jacksonians everywhere, reinforced the position of those who argued that the President's system was simple spoilsmanship. "I hold to your doctrine fully," Swartwout wrote, "that no d——d rascal who made use of his office or its profits for the purpose of keeping Mr. Adams in, and General Jackson out of power, is entitled to the least lenity or mercy, save that of hanging. . . . Whether or not I shall get any thing in the general scramble for plunder, remains to be proven; but I rather guess I shall. . . . Your man, if you want a place, is — —. . . . Make your suit to him, then, and you will get what you want.''

Cadaverous, vacant-eyed, slack-jawed, Swartwout did in fact get his share of the plunder. He was an old friend of Jackson's and one of the President's earliest supporters in New York City. Swartwout wanted to be Collector of the Customs House in New York because that was where much "loot" could be found. The President obligingly gave him the job, but not before Van Buren protested vigorously. Swartwout was a crook, he told the President, who would surely bring disgrace to the administration if given such a sensitive and lucrative post. But one of Jackson's most outstanding characteristics was his fierce loyalty to friends (as well as ferocious animosity toward enemies) and so he refused to believe Van Buren or remove Swartwout. A few years later it was discovered that Swartwout had stolen over a million dollars from the Customs House. He fled to Europe to escape capture and imprisonment. Jackson was deeply offended by his friend's betrayal. "Can he live after this?" he raged, "or will he cut his own throat?"

The Swartwout incident confirmed in the minds of critics that the Jackson administration had inaugurated a spoils system by which the government was being plundered by political hacks as a reward for services rendered the party. "The government," stormed one man, "formerly served by the *elite* of the nation, is now served, to a very considerable extent, by its refuse."

Despite the criticism and the few scandals that surfaced during his administration, Jackson kept insisting that rotation was basically democratic and consistent with the nation's republican form of government. The old system of appointments and removals meant a policy of "elitist" control of the government, said Jackson, and he was more than ever convinced of the need for rotation.

But the furor over the spoils system convinced most Americans that the President had indeed instituted democratic government for the nation. Whether true or not, that's what they believed. To the ordinary citizen, the common man, it seemed that "the people" themselves had finally assumed control of their government. No wonder, then, that this period of American history came to be designated "The Rise of the Common Man." It dovetailed perfectly with remembered scenes of Jackson's inauguration when thousands of "plain folk" converged on Washington to witness the commencement of the "People's government."

Democratic politicians and newspapermen, quite naturally, propagated this notion. Their newspapers rang with claims that Jackson and his party represented the great masses of the electorate and that their victory terminated rule by the "elite." And who were the elite? They were the few, the wellborn, the "aristocracy." They were the rich who had controlled the government long enough. Their day was now over, and their places assumed by the common people. Democracy had arrived in America!

Whether democracy had *really* come to America can be debated. In fact many present-day historians have gone to great pains to prove the phrase "Jacksonian Democracy" a contradiction in terms. But they miss the important point. The people at the time *believed* democracy had come to America and they believed it in part because it was repeated to them over and over, especially during the furor over removals. Thus, one of the important accomplishments of the politicians of the Jacksonian age was the democratic style and tone they generated, even though true democracy for all Americans—including women, blacks, and Indians—was a long way off.

Actually, the rotation system as practiced at this time did not remotely resemble what was described by either the friends or the enemies of Jackson's administration. Its true history was something else. First of all, Jackson did not introduce the system. There was nothing new to removing men from office who were the appointees of one's political opponents. That had been going on for years. Every intelligent man knew this. Even John Quincy Adams's Postmaster General admitted it. "For an administration to bestow its patronage without distinction of party is to court its own destruction." Nevertheless, Jackson's critics honestly contended that his removals were so massive that he had, indeed, invented a spoils system. But here again they were wrong. There never was a purge, never a bloodletting, never a reign of terror. In fact, by no definition was Jackson a spoilsman. Only 919 out of 10,093 government employees were removed during the first eighteen months of his administration. For the entire eight years of his presidency a little more than ten percent of all officeholders were replaced. When these figures are considered in light of normal replacements due to death and resignation or those whose contracts had expired, plus people dismissed for incompetence and dishonesty, they constitute a very creditable record. Certainly this does not represent the actions of a spoilsman who wants to remove everyone in sight and replace him with his friends.

In fact there were many instances when Jackson refused to permit the removal of particular individuals for political reasons. One that received considerable publicity involved Solomon Van Rensselaer. Van Buren had him removed as postmaster of Albany, New York, because he had a long record of political hostility to Van Buren's Regency. Van Rensselaer came to Washington to complain to Jackson, and caught up with the President at a dinner in the White House.

"Sir," said Van Rensselaer to the President, "I have been removed as postmaster of Albany but there is something I wish to show you." With that Van Rensselaer began unbuttoning his jacket.

"What are you doing, Sir?" said the startled Jackson.

"I want you to see my wounds, Sir, received while defending my country against the British during the late war. And my thanks is removal from my office, the only position I have to sustain me in my old age."

Jackson's response was immediate. "Button your jacket," he commanded. "You are still the postmaster."

80

OFFICE HUNTERS FOR THE YEAR 1834.

A highly effective political cartoon lambasts Jackson, the demon, for corrupting the nation by dangling political plums in front of office seekers who twist, turn and jump to grab at electoral spoils.

When Van Buren heard he had been overruled, he went to Jackson to protest. He explained to the President that Van Rensselaer had been a serious and persistent political enemy in the state capital and would use the office to their disadvantage. But Jackson was adamant. "That man has taken British lead in his body. I will not remove him."

It made a pretty story when it got out, and it proved to the American people once more that a patriot, a noble and just man, was President of the United States.

If removals were relatively few, then was the notion that the common people had taken over the operation of government nothing but political propaganda? Not exactly—although the propaganda didn't hurt. As a matter of fact the government was indeed democratized—or opened to a larger number of Americans—but not through a system of removals or rotation.* The infusion of new employees to government service resulted from a vastly increased government payroll. Over a ten-year period, from approximately the middle of the 1820s through most of Jackson's two terms, government expenditures doubled from eleven and a half million dollars per annum to nearly twenty-three million. And much of the distribution of new jobs thus created was in fact carefully controlled and managed by skillful Democrats. For example, the Constitution requires that a census be taken every ten years, and the 1830 census became an excellent opportunity to strengthen the party through the appointment of census takers. Amos Kendall was largely responsible for the superb manner in which the Democrats realized the possibility of gaining popular favor. As early as 1829 he was instructing state leaders about the necessity of building a strong party apparatus at the local level. The initial step in any organizational plan, he advised, should be a "private meeting" of members of the legislature with "all the good and true men" in the state, plus the appointment of a central committee and the designation of "trusty agents in every county." And, in selecting these trusty agents, he went on, "you may hold out to them the hope, that if they are active in organizing and training the party, they will probably receive the appointment to take in the census, and efficient means must be taken to reserve it to them, thus proving that fidelity to the cause shall not go without its reward."

As thousands of new faces joined the government service, small

---

*One modern study (see Further Reading) argues that in terms of education and social standing, Jackson's appointments were little different from John Adams's and Thomas Jefferson's.

wonder then that Jackson's enemies presumed there had been a massive execution of incumbent officeholders.

Although the spoils controversy during Jackson's administration may appear insignificant to us today, actually it was extremely important. Its importance gets to the very heart of government. First of all, in raising the issue Jackson hoped to establish the principle of rotation as a means of strengthening democratic government. Its discussion, pro and con, added to the general climate of democracy that characterized the age. It seemed to document the notion that popular government had been established. As Jackson said—and it has not been said better—office is created for the benefit of the people, not the support of officeholders. Next, in practical terms, the great expansion of the personnel of the government during the 1830s meant many more people were actually engaged in the operation of government. This was a healthy development. So, in fact, Jackson's objective—to draw fresh blood into the government—was at least partly achieved. Finally, and perhaps most important of all, the spoils question directly confronted the problem of how and by whom the government should be run. Jackson offered one way. He called it "rotation." But his way can, and in time did, lead to abuses when it was made to serve only the party and not the people, and when incompetents and criminals took charge of the government's business.

To reformers of the late nineteenth century, the abuses resulting from Jackson's way were solved by civil-service legislation. But that way also created problems. Where will the two major parties—upon whom the country is absolutely dependent for its governmental functions— obtain the means to operate if the patronage is denied them? The answer is obvious. They will turn to the rich, both individual and corporate. And, as the 1970s' scandals of the Nixon administration—the Watergate, milk-fund, selling of ambassadorships, and ITT affairs— surely demonstrated, that alternative is a dangerous and frightening one.

The problem remains. Its importance is clear. Any government can be subverted by its servants. Perhaps the solution lies in getting a great many more people to contribute their time and modest sums to keep the two parties operating honestly and efficiently. If, in time, this does happen, then the Jacksonian objective of drawing the people and their government closer together will have been achieved.

6

The Problem of Union

THE ONLY ISSUE that ever seriously endangered the safety of the Union was slavery. In 1861 the Civil War finally fissured the nation and, in the prophetic words of Daniel Webster, "drenched [the land] in fraternal blood." The scar of that rupture remained red and angry for decades. Indeed, the full consequence of that unhappy era in terms of racial strife remains to this day.

The first serious explosion in the country over slavery occurred during Jackson's administration. But because of Jackson's strong presidential leadership, a willingness on both sides to compromise, and a desire to "save the Union," bloody conflict and secession were prevented, at least temporarily. But as historian William W. Freehling has pointed out, the controversy that erupted in 1832 during Jackson's administration was a "prelude" to the convulsion that shattered the nation thirty years later. When war finally came many Americans wistfully looked back to the Age of Jackson and remembered how their President had guided the country away from secession and its bloody consequence. They wished somehow to summon him from the grave. So, in the presidential election of 1860, many of them went to the polls and voted for Jackson, even though it was foolish and a bit crazy. Maybe they thought that act of desperation would express their need for his kind of leadership and would somehow rescue them from their predicament.

The controversy that boiled out of the Jackson era occurred a little over forty years after the creation of the American nation, and seriously raised questions about the continuance of the Union. But the problem was not a simple one. It got all tangled up with related issues such as the personal ambitions of rival politicians, sectional antagonisms, the antislavery crusade in the North and the anger and hostility that that crusade engendered in the slaveholding South, states' rights and nullification ideas, and the problem of the tariff. To understand what happened in this first crisis over preserving the Union, it is necessary to examine a few of these tangled strands in more detail.

Take political rivalries—the jealousies and opposing ambitions of men who were competing to become Jackson's successor as President.

John C. Calhoun, the spokesman for Southern interests, had been elected Vice-President as Jackson's running mate in 1828, and it seemed to him and to a great many other people, especially his friends, that he would succeed Jackson in the White House in four or eight years, depending on whether the President wanted one or two terms in office. But almost immediately he ran afoul of the presidential ambitions of Martin Van Buren. This, plus his own foolish mistakes, eventually alienated him from Jackson and the Democratic party and drove him to words and deeds that endangered the Union.

When Jackson appointed Van Buren Secretary of State, Calhoun suddenly saw his rival rise up before him. To cut the Secretary back to size, Calhoun embarked on a desperate scheme to force the dismissal of Jackson's cabinet and arrange the appointment of a new cabinet which would exclude Van Buren and his friends. He went about it by attempting to goad the Secretary of War, John Eaton, into resigning; once Eaton was got rid of, it would be easy to push out the rest. Calhoun's scheme went like this: Eaton's wife, Margaret (Peggy) O'Neale Timberlake, had an unsavory past, and Calhoun and his wife set out to embarrass Eaton by deliberately snubbing Peggy. As the soul of Southern propriety and rectitude, Calhoun, and his wife, refused to socialize with her, and they prevailed upon their friends, those both inside and outside the cabinet, to follow their example. This kind of pressure was expected to drive the Eatons from Washington.

But Calhoun's plot backfired. While Van Buren went out of his way to associate with the Eatons, Jackson defended Peggy, seeing in her something of his beloved Rachel, whose life had been shortened, he said, because of similar treatment. "What divine right," Jackson stormed, "let females . . . establish a secrete [sic] inquisition and decree who shall, & who shall not, come into society—and who shall be sacraficed [sic] by their secrete slanders." Eventually Eaton did resign because of the embarrassment, and the entire cabinet was, in fact, replaced, all of which acutely distressed Jackson because it made him and his administration look foolish.

For this he had Calhoun to thank, and he did not take it kindly. He soon discovered additional reasons to resent his Vice-President. Jackson learned that years before, Calhoun, as Secretary of War in the Monroe administration, had sought his censure because of the Florida invasion. It is not particularly clear how Jackson first learned the truth. There had been rumors for years. But all along the General thought Calhoun had been his defender who had tried to block the censure efforts inside Monroe's cabinet. Now in 1830 he learned differently. He was given documentary evidence that showed what Calhoun had really done. Jackson confronted Calhoun with the evidence and asked for an explanation. Responding in a fifty-two-page letter, Calhoun sputtered a defense which left no doubt that he had been guilty of a gross hypocrisy. The President replied with a curt, "No further communication with you on the subject is necessary." Calhoun then made the further mistake of going public with the controversy, printing copies of letters by the various participants, and ending up by accusing Van Buren of reviving the incident in order to stab him in the back and replace him as Jackson's successor in the White House. The public disclosure of these letters infuriated the President because it was calculated to injure his reputation with the people. But friends assured him the Vice-President did himself more harm than anyone else.

As his political fortunes plunged, as his presidential prospects dimmed, Calhoun became reckless—reckless particularly about slavery, for he had nothing to lose. Always in the background, smoldering behind many political debates of the day, lurked the dread issue of slavery. And now Calhoun chose to concentrate on that issue and force a public discussion of it. In the past, in defending the South and what he called its "peculiar institution"—slavery—he had disguised his identity. Now, his immediate presidential hopes dashed, he was openly arguing Southern "rights," particularly the extreme idea of the right of a state to void or nullify any federal law that jeopardized its interests, whatever those interests might be.

Congress passed a particularly high tariff bill in 1828, which was immediately dubbed the Tariff of Abominations and generated cries of secession from the Union by some Southern hotheads. Calhoun returned to his plantation in South Carolina burdened with the need to do something about what he called the "illegality" of forcing such federal legislation as the new tariff down the throat of a reluctant state. He felt he must articulate a theory by which a state could protect itself against the tyranny of the central government. In short, he must devise a method whereby the minority could defend itself against an overbearing majority.

What finally resulted was a paper entitled "Exposition and Protest," which was passed in 1828 by the South Carolina legislature without mentioning the author's name. In it Calhoun not only condemned protective tariffs, but, more importantly, developed the doctrine of nullification. This theory argued that if the federal government passed legislation detrimental to the interests of a state—a tariff, for example—then the state could pass its own law declaring the federal law inoperative within its boundaries. Thus federal legislation would be "nullified" within that state. If three-fourths of all the states nullified, then the law would be void everywhere, just as if the Constitution had been amended. Through the process of nullification, Calhoun argued, the rights of the minority would be protected. In a republic, he said, majority rule must always be tempered by minority rights.

But suppose the federal government refused to allow its laws to be nullified by a single state? Then, said Calhoun—and he said it reluctantly—the state had the right to secede from the Union. But, he insisted, he had advanced the doctrine of nullification to *prevent* secession, to prevent the dismemberment of the Union.

Some of these ideas got a thorough public and national review when a stormy debate broke out in the U.S. Senate in January 1830. Daniel Webster of Massachusetts and Calhoun's spokesman, Robert Y. Hayne of South Carolina, verbally tangled over the composition and nature of the Union.

This historic Webster-Hayne debate was provoked by a resolution restricting the further sale of public lands. But almost immediately the debate moved from the question of public lands and sectional rivalries to the all-embracing questions of the continuance of the Union and the troubling problem of slavery.

In a closely argued and meticulously constructed speech, Hayne defended slavery, states' rights, and Calhoun's doctrine of nullification.

If the Union is to be maintained, Hayne argued, the rights of the South, particularly the right to continue owning slaves, must be respected, and any effort to jeopardize those rights would necessitate some extreme form of state action, nullification first, secession if nullification failed. The idea of nullification was based on viewing the Union as simply a confederation of independent states. Thus, Hayne argued, each state was sovereign within its own boundaries and not absolutely subject to federal law. His speech was so powerful, so logical in its arguments—given its premise about the composition of the Union—that Webster, in composing his "reply," was offered assistance by one justice of the Supreme Court. But Webster was confident and waved the assistance aside. "I shall grind him into a powder," Webster said of Hayne, "and blow him away."

The Senate was packed with spectators to hear the "Godlike Daniel." They filled the gallery and spilled over onto the Senate floor itself. It was quite unusual, if not startling, to see women seated on the same floor with the august body of Senators, adding a touch of color to the surroundings with their bright bonnets and stylish dresses.

Once the upper house had been called to order, Webster rose to seek recognition. The presiding officer, Vice-President Calhoun, recognized him, and the drama was under way.

Webster always began a speech slowly, his right hand resting on his desk, his left hanging limply at his side. The magnificent head would then start to turn from side to side to catch the attention of all the spectators in the gallery, his bushy eyebrows and deep-set eyes producing a hypnotic gaze that held his audience in a paralytic grip. Once he had launched into his speech, his voice would swell with emotion for dramatic effect at one moment and then diminish to a whisper to underscore his meaning at the next. As he became more animated his left hand would work itself behind his back and reach under his coattail, while his right hand swung through the air in great looping gestures as though he were trying to pull his audience closer to him. At one point in this speech Webster directly attacked Hayne's states' rights and nullification positions, saying: "I go for the Constitution as it is, and for the Union as it is. It is, Sir, the people's Constitution, the people's government, made for the people, made by the people, and answerable to the people."

Government for and by the people! Never mind the states and their

88

rights. It is the people who count. The people, indivisible, under the *federal* government.

The speech went on for two days. It reached a peak of high drama that electrified the gallery when Webster shook his finger at Vice-President Calhoun and roared that the Union was composed of people, not states. Then came the overwhelming climax, a statement so noble and true that even today it has the power to move a reader and say something important about the life of the nation. "While the Union lasts," he said, "we have high, exciting, gratifying prospects spread out before us, for us and our children. Beyond that I seek not to penetrate the veil. God grant that in my day, at least, that curtain may not rise! God grant that on my vision never may be opened what lies behind! When my eyes shall be turned to behold for the last time the sun in heaven, may I not see him shining on the broken and dishonored fragments of a once glorious Union; on States dissevered, discordant, belligerent; on a land rent with civil feuds, or drenched, it may be, in fraternal blood! Let their last feeble and lingering glance rather behold the gorgeous ensign of the republic, now known and honored throughout the earth, still full high advanced, its arms and trophies streaming in their original lustre, not a stripe erased or polluted nor a single star obscured, bearing for its motto no such miserable interrogatory as 'What is all this worth?' nor those other words of delusion and folly, 'Liberty first and Union afterwards'; but everywhere, spread all over in characters of living light, blazing on all its ample folds, as they float over the sea and over the land, and on every wind under the whole heavens, that other sentiment, dear to every true American heart—Liberty *and* Union, now and forever, one and inseparable!"

Liberty *and* Union! You can't have one without the other, said Webster. Without Union there is no liberty for anyone. If a state can nullify a federal law, it can crack the Union. And once the Union is cracked, it will split again and again until the United States becomes nothing more than a collection of petty sovereignties. In this weakened condition the nation would be subjected to European domination.

It was a stupendous speech, everyone agreed to that; but leaders of both parties were quite disturbed over this sudden public quarrel concerning the nature of the Union and the place of slavery within American society. If allowed to continue, it would certainly worsen the already tense situation in the mounting sectional wrangling and cause serious

89

rifts within the country. In consultation with Van Buren, Jackson quickly recognized his duty to put a stop to it. He abhorred the idea of nullification. As an intense nationalist he rejected it out of hand. As President he felt he must make his position clear to both Congress and the American people.

Jackson got his opportunity on April 13, 1830, when the Democrats held a commemorative celebration to honor the birthday of Thomas Jefferson. After receiving his invitation to the dinner he conferred with Van Buren, who urged him to let the members of his party know—and that included the nullifiers—that the Union must not be threatened or endangered. It was rumored that the friends of Calhoun—and perhaps Calhoun himself—planned to use the occasion to enlist the support of other states in their extreme interpretation of states' rights. Jackson agreed with Van Buren that the time had arrived to stop them. He went to the dinner exhilarated with a sense of impending battle.

The dinner was held at the Indian Queen Hotel. A full portrait of George Washington and two busts of Thomas Jefferson decorated the hall. Numerous evergreens were placed around the room. The diners sat at two parallel tables, with a cross table at the head "which promoted festivity and sociality." When the dinner ended the President was asked to give a toast. Jackson rose and lifted his glass. Then slowly his gaze moved from person to person as though he were looking for someone in particular. Indeed, he was. When the eyes of everyone in the room were riveted on him, Jackson turned and stared directly at John C. Calhoun. Raising his glass a bit higher, he fired his volley squarely into the face of the nullifier.

"Our *Federal* Union," he cried: "*It must be preserved.*"

Utter silence gripped his listeners. His intent and meaning were thunderously clear.

The Vice-President followed with his toast. "The Union," Calhoun declared: "Next to our liberty, the most dear; may we all remember that it can only be preserved by respecting the rights of the States and distributing equally the benefit and burden of the Union." Then came the political master, Martin Van Buren. "Mutual forbearance and reciprocal concession," he said: "Through their agency the Union was established. The patriotic spirit from which they emanated will forever sustain it."

As far as Jackson was concerned, Calhoun's public avowal of nullification had separated him from the community of men dedicated to the defense and preservation of the federal Union. Calhoun's words and

In later life, Calhoun's obsession with the need to protect slavery and the rights of the South gave him this staring, somber look.

actions, he felt, were motivated by his selfish needs and political ambition. The Vice-President was willing to sacrifice party and country for self-serving ends. His present course, wrote Jackson, proved "Calhoun a *villain*."

Just how far Calhoun was prepared to go to demonstrate his independence—and in party terms, disloyalty—became evident shortly after Jackson re-formed his cabinet. The President appointed Van Buren minister to Great Britain, but when the Senate voted on confirmation the result was a tie, 23 to 23, with Southern nullifiers joining Clay, Webster, and other National Republicans in voting against confirmation. The tie-breaking vote lay with the Vice-President, John C. Calhoun.

The angry man could not resist the temptation to strike at his rival. Hating Van Buren and tormented by a need for revenge, Calhoun voted to reject the nomination, even though it meant calling down on his head the wrath of Jackson and the other Democratic leaders. After casting his vote, Calhoun turned to a friend and said, "It will kill him, sir, kill him dead. He will never kick sir, never kick." True, Calhoun had killed a minister, but at the same time he effectively removed himself as Jackson's successor to the presidency—a removal, as it turned out, that proved permanent.

Jackson immediately notified party leaders that he wanted Van Buren as his vice-presidential running mate when he sought reelection to the presidency in 1832. "I have no hesitation in saying that Calhoun is one of the most base hypocritical and unprincipled villains in the United States," said Jackson. He wrote Van Buren that his rejection was a personal attack on the executive, which "the people will properly resent . . . by placing you in the chair of the very man whose casting vote rejected you."

Calhoun was now beyond the pale. Even as Vice-President he no longer counted in Jackson-dominated Democratic circles. He was without a party. His national leadership was gone. As such he became an extremely dangerous man, a man intent on one thing—the interests of his section, the South. And that meant slavery. Every skill he had, every intellectual tool he possessed, was now concentrated on the protection and defense of the South's "peculiar institution." John C. Calhoun would hasten the rush toward confrontation between the North and South.

But apart from the rivalries of ambitious politicians as a factor in opening up the slavery controversy and thereby endangering the Union, two other extremely important developments took place during the 1820s and 1830s that set the North and South on a collision course. Simultaneously, there arose a great demand in the North to end slavery, while in the South there was a rising determination to preserve slavery at all costs.

The antislavery mood in the North had been building for decades. Even in the colonial period there had been opposition to the institution, particularly among Quakers. By the 1770s and 1780s, most of New England had declared slavery illegal, with New York, Pennsylvania, and New Jersey following in the 1780s and 1790s. In the Northwest Territory (the area which later became the states of Michigan, Ohio, Indiana, Illinois, and Wisconsin) the Northwest Ordinance of 1787 forbade slavery; and in 1820, as part of the Missouri Compromise, it was prohibited north of 36° 30' in the Louisiana Purchase. Furthermore, the Constitution permitted Congress to terminate the importation of slaves— though only after 1808.

This small beginning of the antislavery crusade received a jolting thrust forward during the Jacksonian era. The fact that most western European nations had abandoned slavery had a profound impact on Americans. England abolished the institution in the 1830s, and all the Latin American countries, with the exception of Cuba and Brazil, emancipated their slaves. That a supposedly advanced, civilized, modern and democratic society like the United States could still tolerate the "peculiar institution" in the middle of the nineteenth century seemed monstrous to most Northern liberals.

In the 1820s vocal denunciation of slavery erupted across the tier of Northern states. Several newspapers were founded with the specific purpose of advancing the cause of emancipation by stirring up public opinion over the horror and savagery of the slave institution. In the same way that politicians were founding newspapers to create and control voting majorities, abolitionists were imitating the technique to start a movement that would purge the nation of the brutal institution. The first important paper was the *Genius of Universal Emancipation*. It was a Baltimore journal whose editor, Benjamin Lundy, complemented his writing against slavery by organizing antislavery societies. Lundy was especially active in his organizing work, and indeed the abolitionist crusade might never have succeeded as well as it ultimately did without the intensive effort devoted to organizing people into formal groups, collecting money, and providing abolitionist propaganda that was circulated around the country. Like party politicians, abolitionists organized themselves into militant cadres to slay the slavery beast.

Lundy's newspaper was founded in 1821, and in it he urged the use of reason in persuading Southerners to abandon the slave system. He did not advocate involving the federal government to solve the problem. Soon, however, a more strident editorial voice was heard. William Lloyd Garrison, who learned his trade by writing for Lundy, believed in a more aggressive approach to abolition. His was a raucous, fiery voice demanding the *immediate* end of slavery. His radicalism—he went to prison on one occasion—brought about an estrangement from Lundy. Garrison moved to Boston, where in 1831 he founded his *Liberator* newspaper, the mood and tone of which were sounded with the first issue. "I am aware," Garrison editorialized, "that many object to the severity of my language; but is there not cause for severity? I *will be* as harsh as truth, and as uncompromising as justice. On this subject, I do not wish to think, or speak, or write, with moderation. No! No! Tell a man whose house is on fire, to give a moderate alarm; tell him to moderately rescue his wife from the hands of the ravisher; tell the mother to gradually extricate her babe from the fire into which it has fallen—but urge me not to use moderation in a cause like the present. I am in earnest—I will not equivocate—I will not excuse—I will not retreat a single inch—AND I WILL BE HEARD."

The fact that the Constitution of the United States recognized slavery—it allowed three-fifths of the slaves to be counted in determining each state's representation in the House of Representatives, did not allow Congress to restrict the importation of slaves until 1808, and provided for returning fugitive slaves to their masters—only proved to Garrison how basically evil the American political system really was. Indeed, he called the Constitution "an agreement with hell and a covenant with death." This denunciation of the supreme law of the land, during a period of intense nationalism in which the signers of the Declaration and the framers of the Constitution were virtually deified, did not help the antislavery cause in the North. There were some Americans—even ardent abolitionists—who regarded Garrison as an extremist, a radical, a lunatic, whose sole purpose was the destruction of the American system of government.

What they especially disliked was the physical violence that began to attend the crusade. The mood was turning ugly. Frequently, at antislavery meetings, abolitionists lost their tempers and insulted the country or jeered at prominent men of the past, like Washington and

Jefferson, who had owned slaves. Sometimes fistfights broke out when anti-abolitionists attended the meetings to foment trouble. Bricks, stones, and other missiles were hurled at people. Garrison himself was roughed up and dragged through the streets by a Boston mob who resented his attack on the Constitution. And Elijah P. Lovejoy, an abolitionist newspaperman, was murdered by a mob in Alton, Illinois, in 1837.

To advance immediate abolition throughout the United States, Garrison had founded the New England Anti-Slavery Society in 1832, and a year later the American Anti-Slavery Society, a national organization to coordinate and direct efforts to end slavery. Among the most notable men and women who were drawn to the abolitionist crusade were Theodore Dwight Weld, Wendell Phillips, Lewis and Arthur Tappan, Gerrit Smith, and Sarah and Angelina Grimké, two sisters from an aristocratic, slave-owning South Carolina family who had moved to the North because of their intense hatred of slavery. Weld became the Anti-Slavery Society's most pungent publicist and lecturer. Angelina Grimké, his wife, was of enormous help, particularly in gathering materials from newspapers to document the horrors of slavery, and in her fervent speeches on the lecture circuit advocating abolition.

Thanks to the organization, agitation, lecturing, and publishing of these converted, conscientious, devoted, and dedicated abolitionists, the antislavery movement spread rapidly throughout the North, heating up the political climate and generating an atmosphere of controversy. But not everyone was a Garrisonian. Not all were extremists. In fact, most Americans who had any antislavery feelings at all did not advocate immediate emancipation. They preferred a systematic, orderly, slow freeing of slaves, extended over a period of years in which the slave owners would be financially compensated for their loss. They feared that the sudden termination of the slave system would cause many social and economic problems for the entire nation. Others would go no further than opposing the extension of slavery into the territories of the United States. Probably they had no regard for black people and were motivated by a selfish economic desire to restrict the territories to free (white) labor. And there were other Northerners who were downright opposed to abolition. Many of these were poor whites living in Northern cities who hated the freed black men because they competed with them for available (usually unskilled) jobs. Therefore they wished to keep the blacks in bondage.

The danger, apparent to every responsible political leader in both

One of the horrors of slavery was the auction block. A mother and infant are being sold to the highest bidder. Behind, the flag of the Republic, symbolizing the ''land of the free,'' makes a mockery of American democracy.

parties, was that the issue of slavery might suddenly blow up the country, as Garrison and other extremists seemed to be advocating. This catastrophe had to be avoided at all costs. The essential task, as most politicians saw it, was to hold the Union together. This they understood. This they saw very clearly. They were not trying to protect slavery, though many of them were socially conservative, unconcerned about the plight of the slaves. That they recognized their duty as politicians to preserve the Union did not mean they advocated slavery; it did not mean that national politics was ruled by proslavery sentiment. The key phrase had been sounded by Jackson: "Our Federal Union: It must be preserved." Nevertheless, extremist abolitionists in the North were watching their opportunity to detonate their bomb.

There were extremists in the South, too.

The rise of the abolitionist movement naturally roused white Southerners to a defense of their way of life. At the time of the drafting of the Constitution it had not been uncommon to find many Southerners apologetic about slavery, declaring the institution moribund and certain to die in the immediate future through a natural evolutionary process. But the evolutionary process took a different direction. At the beginning of the nineteenth century the South experienced an economic transformation that locked it permanently to the slave system. The invention of the cotton gin in 1793 by Eli Whitney, a Connecticut Yankee, provided the transformation by revolutionizing cotton processing. Now both short-haired and long-haired cotton could be grown profitably all over the South, not simply along the Atlantic coastal area. Cotton thus became the staple of the entire South, its cash crop. And growing cotton necessitated a large work force in the fields, which Southerners argued could be satisfied only by the slave system. It is interesting to note that cotton production from 1790 to 1810—a twenty-year span—rose from 3,000 bales a year to 178,000 bales and that the number of slaves in the South during the same period jumped from 700,000 to 1,200,000. The percentage of cotton exported tripled during this same period. By the 1830s approximately half the nation's total exports consisted of one commodity: cotton.

This economic dependence upon slavery, plus the mounting attacks by abolitionists, converted white Southerners from apologists for, to defenders of, the "peculiar institution." By the Jacksonian era they had completely abandoned their previous and more ambiguous position. Gone was the apology, gone the ambiguity. John C. Calhoun now

98

argued that slavery was "a positive good." Southern clergymen now cited the Bible to prove divine approval of the system. Throughout history, argued one defender, all great civilizations were based on slavery. It was practically the *sine qua non* for material and cultural progress. "At the slaveholding South all is peace, quiet, plenty and contentment," wrote another. "We have no mobs, no trades unions, no strikes for higher wages, no armed resistance to the law, but little jealousy of the rich by the poor." Not only that, "there is no rivalry, no competition to get employment among slaves, as among free laborers. Nor is there a war between master and slave. . . . The institution of slavery gives full development and full play to the affections."

Thus, at the very moment that abolitionism was spreading in the North and throughout the world, a determination to perpetuate slavery gripped the South. And as abolitionist propaganda increased in volume and effectiveness, slave owners grew more and more apprehensive, defensive, angry—and frightened. Many Southern whites lived in communities where they were outnumbered by blacks, sometimes by twenty to one. They lived in fear and dread that black men one day would rise up in fury and massacre all whites, just as had occurred a few years before on the island of Santo Domingo in the Caribbean. Southerners became so fearful of this possibility that they were suspicious of everything said, done, or even remotely suggested about their slaves.

There were just enough slave insurrections to make Southern fears something more than illusion. One was the Denmark Vesey Conspiracy that had occurred in Charleston, South Carolina, in 1822. Vesey was a free mulatto who, with Gullah Jack, an old African witch doctor, supposedly convinced thousands of blacks to murder all white men in Charleston and rape their women. Actually not more than a hundred slaves were involved and it is doubtful the conspiracy was ever a serious one. Nevertheless, word of a "servile insurrection" spread among slave owners and immediately five companies of South Carolina soldiers were called out. There were many arrests and during the next two months thirty-five slaves were hanged and another thirty-seven banished from the state. The "conspiracy" crushed, Charleston slave owners breathed a sigh of relief. They were certain they had barely escaped the horrors of rape, murder and theft. "Let this never be forgotten," wrote one man, "that our NEGROES . . . are the *anarchists* and the *domestic enemy*; the *common enemy of civilized society*, and the barbarians who would, IF THEY COULD, become the DESTROYERS *of our race*."

99

In the next few years there were several other slave disturbances, none serious but all frightening Southerners half out of their wits. Then, in 1831, came the Nat Turner Rebellion. This was a major uprising, the most important slave insurrection in American history. And this knocked the Southerners into a perpetual state of shock and terror.

Nat Turner, with nearly a hundred slaves, murdered about sixty whites—more than half of them women and children—in Virginia. Turner was a remarkable man. In the minds of some, a religious fanatic. He had a dream, a messianic dream that he was destined to save his people, to free his fellow slaves. But such dreams often lead to violence, deliberate or not. In Turner's case it was deliberate.

The revolt he led happened at a place appropriately called Jerusalem in southeast Virginia along the North Carolina border. It started on Sunday, August 22, 1831. Within a day almost all the white men, women, and children of this quiet rural area were slaughtered. As the slaves moved from farm to farm they gathered guns, swords, and other weapons. Only one white family is known to have survived. They were spared, said Turner in his *Confession*, because they "thought no better of themselves than they did of the negroes."

As soon as the alarm was sounded, heavy reinforcements of the local constabulary rushed to the area and suppressed the rebellion. There was a savage massacre. Slaves were killed on the spot, without arrest and without trial. Members of a vigilante group swore they would kill "every black person they saw in Southampton County." A contingent of black prisoners was summarily beheaded by one military unit and the heads placed on poles for the edification and instruction of other slaves. It is not known how many blacks were butchered in the massacre— possibly several hundred.

The horror of this killing—of whites by blacks, not the other way around, of course—swept the South. "Fear was seen in every face," went one North Carolina report, "women pale and terror-stricken, children crying out for protection, men fearful and full of foreboding." This hysteria completed the radicalization of many Southerners. Now more than ever they defended slavery and their particular way of life. They would not countenance criticism of any sort. They insisted abolitionists be silenced lest they trigger additional insurrections.

In such a tense and emotionally charged situation there was always the danger that a simple incident or a seemingly trivial event might touch off an explosion that would permanently damage the nation.

It was not long in coming. On the surface it did not appear that slavery was involved. But it was there. It was always there, lurking, subtly poisoning everything that was taking place.

The event that started the rush toward confrontation began in 1832 as a dispute over the tariff. But it quickly developed into a controversy that raised again the doctrine of nullification and threatened to lead to Southern secession. It brought the nation close to war.

Since the early 1820s, the tariff had been a source of irritation and discord between the North and South. Passage of a tariff on imported manufactures was almost guaranteed to ignite tempers and drive Southerners into "calculating the value of the Union." Their reaction to the Tariff of Abominations in 1828 had proved how dangerous and unpredictably treacherous the issue could be. Party leaders were leery about adjusting the duties in the foreseeable future. Inequitable though some of the rates might be, the country was living with them, and therefore it was monumentally injudicious at this time to fool around with them.

But fool with them they did. Hoping to correct past mistakes, Congress passed the Tariff of 1832. Although it removed some of the abominations of the 1828 law, Congress did not lower the rates to any significant degree. The tariff wall remained relatively high. But many Democrats voted for it on the assumption that an improved bill might quiet passions in the South. Jackson signed it for the same reason. But the nullifiers—men like Calhoun and his friends in South Carolina—were not quieted. On the contrary, they demanded total surrender on the issue, an end to all protective tariffs. All their fears and frustrations, all their concern for slavery, states' rights, and the Southern way of life were now embodied in this single issue. Counting on Southern discontent over tariff rates as support for their contemplated defiance of the government, the nullifiers proceeded to organize themselves in South Carolina to test the ties of union.

In Washington, John C. Calhoun wrote the Governor of South Carolina, James Hamilton, Jr., urging him to apply his doctrine of nullification and declare the new tariff inoperable in South Carolina. "The Union," he wrote, "of which the Constitution is the bond, is a union of States, and not of individuals." A state may declare an act of Congress null and void within its borders, said Calhoun, and this action is binding on all the citizens of the state. Simultaneously, he argued that the federal government had no authority to coerce a state.

101

The restraint Calhoun had once exercised—based on his expectation that he would follow Jackson into the White House, provided of course that he did not alienate Northern sensibilities—was now gone. Van Buren had replaced him as Jackson's successor. Now Calhoun urged radical measures to solve the South's problems. He urged nullification—and, if necessary, secession.

Governor Hamilton called a special session of the state legislature to respond to the "outrage" of the federal government in legislating a new tariff. Acting decisively and under the control of the well-organized nullifiers, the legislature in turn called for an elected convention to meet on November 19, 1832, to act in the name of the state.

The convention, as expected, adopted the ideas of Calhoun and passed an Ordinance of Nullification on November 24, 1832, by a vote of 136 to 26. The Ordinance declared the tariff laws of 1828 and 1832 null and void and forbade the collection of tariff duties within the borders of South Carolina. It went on to warn the federal government that if force were used against the state to require it to obey the law, then South Carolina would quit the Union. Once that happened it was expected the rest of the South would also secede.

President Jackson was shocked and angered by the action of his native state. He believed the "nullies," as they were called, were deliberately baiting him in their desire to cause trouble. But did they not realize, he wrote, that as President he had sworn to uphold the Constitution and faithfully execute the laws of the United States, that his duty was clear, that he had no choice? The tariff was law, and, "by the eternal," he would uphold the law even against the state of his birth. In a Proclamation dated December 10, 1832, he spoke directly to the people of South Carolina. He praised them but he also warned them. He would not tolerate defiance of the national government, he said. "Those who told you that you might peacefully prevent [the] execution [of federal law] deceived you. . . . Their object is disunion. But be not deceived by names. Disunion by armed force is *treason*. Are you really ready to incur its guilt?"

While Jackson tried to warn the people of South Carolina against an illegal act which would force his hand to execute his constitutional duty, he took other more direct actions to prevent possible secession and civil war. First he wrote to known unionists within the state to gain their help and cooperation. In particular he corresponded with Joel R. Poinsett, the former minister to Mexico, who had formed a Union party within the

102

state to oppose the action of the "nullies," especially their secessionist intent. In one letter to Poinsett, Jackson said: "I repeat to the union men [in South Carolina] again, fear not, *the union will be preserved* and treason and rebellion put down, when and where it may shew [*sic*] its monster head."

Jackson also checked out the federal government's military strength just in case it was needed, even for purposes of demonstration. He alerted naval authorities in Norfolk, Virginia, to prepare a squadron to send against South Carolina if the use of force proved necessary. He notified the federal commanders of the several forts in the Charleston harbor to prepare for a possible emergency. And he hurried several thousand troops to the southern border of North Carolina, to move into South Carolina at his command if the state tried to carry forward its defiance of federal law.

Meanwhile, Calhoun resigned as Vice-President on December 28, 1832, a little over two months before his term legally expired. In a complicated maneuver, he got himself elected U.S. Senator by the South Carolina legislature; thus the state's most effective speaker and parliamentarian was stationed inside Congress to protect the state's interests. He replaced Robert Y. Hayne, who was brought home and elected to the Governor's chair. This switching of personnel was expected to demonstrate South Carolina's determination to fight on at every front. Having Calhoun in the Senate meant that the chief nullifier had a national forum whereby he could lambast the federal government, the North, Jackson, the Democratic party, and anyone else who dared to force South Carolina to obey any law she deemed contrary to her interests.

But it was not the tariff that really bothered the South, although clearly such legislation provided a focus for resentment. The real issue was slavery, upon which everything else depended. For that reason the controversy was recognized as a serious and dangerous development which could tear the Union apart.

Fortunately, the politics of brinkmanship attempted by South Carolina and John C. Calhoun were answered by the masterful politics of President Andrew Jackson. His response to the threat of secession was nothing short of brilliant. As he repeatedly said, he was determined to preserve the Union. While he prepared for the possibility of bloodshed he did everything within his power to work out a compromise by which both sides could back off gracefully. Besides aiding and encouraging the unionists within South Carolina to provide a balance to the "nullies" within the state, he went to Congress and urged a policy of conciliation. Henry Clay was one of the first to respond. The Senator from Kentucky, after consulting with a number of Congressmen to find a compromise that would encourage South Carolina to abandon nullification without penalizing Northern interests, introduced a new tariff bill in 1833.

This so-called Compromise Tariff of 1833 provided a ten-year truce—its most important provision—during which time the tariff rates would be slowly reduced. At the same time another bill was passed providing the necessary military assistance to insure obedience to the law. This was called the Force Bill—or, by Southerners, the Bloody Bill.

South Carolina immediately accepted the compromise. Its nullifying convention reassembled on March 11, 1833, and repealed the Ordinance of Nullification against the tariff laws. But then, to save face, it nullified the Force Bill. Since it was a meaningless gesture Jackson allowed South Carolina this conceit. For the sake of the Union he could afford to be generous.

South Carolina retreated from its defiance because the state had tried the doctrine of nullification and found it wanting. Not another Southern state had supported her and she could not risk going it alone. The reason for her isolation most probably was the lack of enthusiasm in the other slaveholding states for nullification. It was a doctrine of dubious validity. But had South Carolina actually seceded—a right held to be fully constitutional by other Southern states—and had the issue been other than economic, it might have been a different story altogether. South Carolina never nullified again. The next time she chose to act, she seceded. And war resulted.

None of the basic problems facing the nation, such as slavery, sectional antagonisms between the North and South, or the constitutional rights of the states vis-à-vis the federal government, were solved by the nullification controversy. What was accomplished through strong executive leadership and a spirit of compromise, which is the very essence of politics, was avoidance of armed conflict and the breakup of the Union. It was a notable achievement. Unfortunately, these ingredients were not present thirty years later when these problems were finally submitted to the test of arms.

7

The Indian Problem

IF PARTY LEADERS during the Jacksonian era failed to solve the problem of slavery, the same can not be said of their handling of the Indian problem. This issue they solved with a vengeance, much to the satisfaction of Americans at the time. But the effects of that solution have had a terrible impact on the nation right down to the present. What is particularly sad is that the solution to the Indian problem was an ugly contradiction to the general democratic mood of the Jacksonian age.

For some modern Americans there is only one word to describe the nation's historic policy toward the Indians: genocide—the calculated, ruthless, seemingly insane determination to exterminate a whole race of people. One modern historian, Bernard W. Sheehan, summed it up when he wrote: "The white man is guilty. He has been charged with the destruction of the American Indian, the evidence has been presented, and the verdict returned for all to see." Another recent historian has observed that it is rather fortunate that our present concern and sympathy for the Indians came when it was too late to do anything about it, too late to reverse the history of a hundred years. If Americans had it to do all over again, he said, most probably they would not hesitate to repeat the policies of the past. After all, the Indians stood in the way of the progress of the majority, could not or would not adapt to the changing society, occupied desired land—in short, failed to become cultural white men. So they had to be eliminated, one way or another.

The concern of many Americans today for the plight of the Indians is properly humane and sympathetic, perhaps a bit romantic, and not a little tinged with an overly simplistic view of history, namely the wicked-white-man interpretation. Somehow, it is assumed, things could have been different had there been decency and respect shown the Indians for their property and cultures. Had the white men been less greedy, less racist in their thinking, had the Indians been better protected, especially by the federal government, the treaties kept, the dishonest agents weeded out and punished, somehow the Indians as Indians could have endured; two cultures or maybe even an intermingling of cultures might have resulted. But it just didn't work out that way—and the reasons say a great deal about the nature of the democracy of the Jacksonian era.

It is interesting to note that not until political democracy was achieved in America—the creation of a mass electorate, the rise of the common man, the respect for the popular will, the notion that political leaders must serve as representatives of the people, and the rest—not until then did the country decide to get rid of its Indians. And it fell to Andrew Jackson, the symbol of the great democracy, to run the Indians off their ancestral lands and dump them unceremoniously in remote and desolate corners of the United States where they barely survived. In order to understand how this calamity occurred it is necessary to understand white-red relations from the very start of the nation's history.

White America's policy from the beginning was a curious mixture of the benign and the malevolent. This contradictory attitude commenced with the arrival of the British in North America. Colonists fluctuated from outright warfare—seizing land and driving the Indians from white society—to missionary endeavor to Christianize the Indians, educate them, share with them the benefits of Western civilization, and welcome them into the white community. Sometimes Indian land was stolen, sometimes legitimately obtained through purchase and treaty.

During the American Revolution, the ambiguous policy of Americans changed. Because most Indians allied themselves with the British, Americans felt justified in punishing the Indians for their mistake of judgment by forced cessions of land. But the Indians resisted this policy—resisted it so successfully that the government was obliged to return to a policy of land purchase to get the cessions it wanted.

Even so, many Americans practiced only one policy toward the Indians: theft and, when necessary, homicide. To them, Indians were inferior. All Americans wanted was their land. They felt the Indians had no rights white men need respect.

When the Constitution was adopted, establishing a government committed to freedom and liberty, the situation of the Indians living within the territorial limits of the United States contradicted the ennobling ideas of both the Declaration of Independence and the Constitution. But the Founding Fathers who won independence from Great Britain and wrote the Constitution lived in what they believed was an Age of Enlightenment. They were convinced that men of reason, intelligence, and goodwill could come together, and in a spirit of compromise and accommodation resolve whatever issues divided or troubled them. They were committed to rational solutions of men's problems. Therefore, they reasoned that Indians were not inferior to white men. In their view, these "noble savages" simply existed on a lower stage of development and one day would catch up to modern society—provided the white man's civilization was brought to them. In exchange for land the Indians would receive the blessings of Western civilization. What could be fairer than that?

Under President George Washington and his Secretary of War, Henry Knox—for it was the War Secretary whose office handled the Indian problem—the national policy of the United States was formulated to "civilize" Indians and absorb them into the Union. Washington said he sought "to advance the happiness of the Indians and to attach them firmly to the United States." He, like others of his time, hoped that with the application of this policy the Indian would "cease his wandering ways," adopt the practice of private property as the white man understood it, farm like white Americans, raise oxen, sheep, and other domestic animals, build comfortable houses, educate his children, and embrace Christianity.

President Thomas Jefferson continued this policy. As he said to a delegation of Indians who visited him in the capital, "Let me entreat you on the lands now given you to begin every man a farm, let him enclose it, cultivate it, build a warm house on it, and when he dies let it belong to his wife and children after him." Like Washington, Jefferson simply ignored the agricultural aspects of Indian society. Both Presidents assumed the Indians knew little, compared to whites, about farming and working the land. Thus, if the Indians would adopt white men's ways, Jefferson said to them, then "you will unite yourselves with us, and we shall all be Americans. You will mix with us by marriage. Your blood will run in our veins and will spread with us over this great island." But if the Indians refused to accept civilization, what then? Why then they were doomed. "We shall be obliged to drive them," said Jefferson, "with the beasts of the forest into the Stony [Rocky] Mountains."

This policy of assimilation or integration of the two races reflected the stubborn hope and belief of the early Presidents. It was quite appropriate to the men of the Age of Enlightenment. But it just didn't work out. For while the United States was making dramatic, even revolutionary advances—a population doubling in ten years, with many new Western states added to the Union, canals and other public works being built so rapidly as to constitute a transportation revolution—with all these accomplishments advancing the prosperity and happiness of the nation, the Indians had remained indifferent to the benefits and opportunities of Western civilization except to adopt its worst vices. They continued their "wandering ways." They refused the invitation to become cultural white men. They were obviously going nowhere, while the white man was pressing further along the road of progress and improvement. Civilization, Americans finally concluded, was simply not meant for the red man. He couldn't handle it.

Though the nation pulsed with democratic spirit during the 1820s and 1830s, the idea of equality was never extended to include Indians. Furthermore, the concept of assimilation between the two races was now reckoned a failure and repeatedly attacked by a number of politicians who seemed to reflect the popular attitude. Henry Clay, for example, as Secretary of State under President Adams, had stated that "it was impossible to civilize Indians. It was not in their nature. They were essentially inferior to the Anglo-Saxon race . . . and their disappearance from the human family will be no great loss to the world." And Henry Clay was not alone. Many Americans agreed with this racist attitude, arguing that the Indians were incapable of self-improvement and only blocked the natural expansion and progress of the civilized white man. There was only one thing to do under the circumstances, and that was to remove this obstacle so that the civilized race could have all the territory it needed to fulfill its destiny.

Removal! Send the tribes out of the country. Send them west. Send

108

them where they would cease to take up valuable land and thus interfere with the nation's growth and development. And the sooner it was done the better.

By the time Andrew Jackson was elected President many Americans demanded an end to Indian presence in white society. As the popularly elected President, the representative of the democracy, Jackson was expected to solve the problem. And from the very start of his administration he indicated a readiness to oblige. In his first annual message to Congress in 1829, Jackson noted that some Southern tribes had attempted to create independent governments within the limits of Georgia and Alabama. But these states extended their laws over the Indians, arguing that the Indians were occupying land within their sovereign jurisdictions. The Indians rejected this argument and appealed to the United States government for protection. They appealed for help to their old enemy, that Indian fighter par excellence, Andrew Jackson.

These Southeastern tribes were not savages. They were not weak aborigines defenseless before aggressive states. The truth of the matter, though few white men cared to acknowledge it, was that some Indian tribes had made real "progress in the arts of civilized life," to quote from Jackson's own message. The President knew this and admitted it. He knew the Southern tribes had made notable advances, especially the Cherokees. Many Cherokees lived in fine houses, cultivated large plantations and even owned slaves—just to prove how "civilized" they really were. They had schools and a newspaper and their own written language. They tended to act like members of an independent, sovereign power, capable of conducting its own affairs. But the trouble was that they occupied land within the boundaries of several states. Indeed, some fifty-three thousand Cherokees, Creeks, Chickasaws and Choctaws extended over thirty-three million acres of land in the southern and southwestern section of the United States east of the Mississippi River.

White men in general, and the states of Georgia and Alabama in particular, were contemptuous of Indian pretensions to civilization and independence. All they knew was that red men blocked their territorial progress by occupying land they wanted. So they insisted on removal— beyond the Mississippi River if possible, below ground if not.

The success of some tribes in adapting to the white man's civilization did not alter the fundamental belief of Americans at this time that Indians generally were inferior and that their disappearance from the

109

human family, as Clay said, would be no great loss. Even men of goodwill, men friendly to Indian rights, men not greedy for Indian land, slowly came to the conclusion that removal or annihilation were the only alternatives facing the Indians. Either they moved west of the Mississippi River and got out of harm's way or they would be buried—literally destroyed—they themselves and their cultures. "Say to the [Indians]," Jackson wrote at this time, "where they now are, they and my white children are too near to each other to live in harmony and peace. Then game is destroyed & many of their people will not work, & till the earth. Beyond the river Mississippi where a part of their nation have gone, their father has provided a country, large enough for them all, and he advises them to remove to it. There, their white brethren will not trouble them . . . and they can live upon it, they and all their children as long as grass grows or water runs in peace and plenty. It will be theirs forever."

Jackson had little choice in deciding on a policy of removal. According to a distinguished historian of American Indian policy, Francis Prucha, the President had only four courses of action open to him. The first choice was to kill the Indians outright. Simply send in the army and by brute force exterminate the race. While many frontiersmen strongly and eagerly approved such a policy, it was never even remotely contemplated by Jackson or any responsible official within his administration.

His second choice was to attempt the assimilation or integration of the white and red races, as the earlier Presidents had anticipated. But by the 1820s it was abundantly clear that this policy was unacceptable. Most white men in America had a long history of racism. They regarded other races as inferior and were not about to accept assimilation, no matter what the Founding Fathers hoped. Consequently, any attempt to mingle the races was foredoomed to failure. Southerners were especially adamant on this point. If assimilation were possible with the red men, would assimilation with the black men be far behind?

Jackson's third choice was to protect the Indians where they lived. They would be islands within white society, safeguarded by treaties, and, necessarily, by military force to keep white men from encroaching on the red men's territory. Those who opposed removal favored this alternative. Even today critics of the removal policy feel some variation of this choice should have been attempted by the American government. But the standing army needed for such an operation against avaricious

110

whites would have been enormous, more than was possible in the 1830s. The country would have become an armed camp.

The fourth choice was removal, and to Jackson this policy was the only answer to the unyielding antagonism that existed between the white and red races. And to a large extent the policy was adopted to protect the Indians and their cultures against inevitable extinction if they stayed where they were. Jackson told Congress that the white man had the means to destroy the Indians unless they moved—and on that score there could be no doubt. "That this fate surely awaits the Indians if they remain within the limits of the States," he said, "does not admit of a doubt. Humanity and national honor demand that every effort should be made to avert so great a calamity."

It is difficult to believe—indeed mind-boggling—that Andrew Jackson, the Indian fighter, the stern commander of the Creek Indian War, actually acted out of concern for the well-being of the Indians and for their civilization. Of course, it is unquestionable that he also responded to what he knew the American people demanded. But he could have sat on his hands, done nothing and let "nature" take its course, which undoubtedly would have meant annihilation for the Indian. Instead, as his private letters and official papers and messages repeated many times, he was most anxious to preserve Indian life and culture, and the only way he felt it could be done was to separate the races—separate them forever.

It has been said that Jackson hated Indians. That it was blind hatred, nothing else, which prompted his action. Those who make this charge forget that he raised an Indian boy from infancy. The infant had been discovered in the arms of his dead mother in 1813 in the Creek village of Tallushatchee after a particularly bloody battle during the Creek War. Jackson had asked other Indian women to care for the boy, but they refused. "All his relations are dead," they said; "kill him too." But the General spurned this advice, named the child Lincoyer, and took him back to the Hermitage, where he raised him and gave him a good education. Unfortunately the boy died of tuberculosis at the age of seventeen. But, if Jackson hated Indians how then did he take one into his home and treat him as a member of the family?

Still, that he did not hate Indians does not mean Jackson was their devoted friend and protector. As President he regarded them as a responsibility, which meant preventing their destruction. So, in 1829, he asked Congress to pass legislation creating an Indian Territory west

111

of the Mississippi River outside the limits of any existing state or territory. This new Territory would be guaranteed to the Indians as long as they occupied it, each tribe having a distinct control over a portion of it. There they could have their own government; they would be subject to no other control from the United States except what was necessary to preserve peace on the frontier and between the several tribes. The emigration would be voluntary, said Jackson, for it would be "as cruel as unjust" to force them "to abandon the graves of their fathers and seek a home in a distant land." But if they did refuse to leave, Jackson warned, then they must be subject to the laws of the states within which they resided. And, in view of the declared intentions of many states, that was a very unpleasant prospect.

The immediate problem was Georgia. That state had already planned to do something about the Indians living within her borders. And the Cherokee Nation was the special target. In December 1829 the state legislature passed a law extending the authority of the state over the lands held by the Indians within her borders. But the Cherokees resisted. Not by brandishing tomahawks. Not by going on the warpath and killing and burning. But by the most "civilized" manner possible: The Cherokees sued Georgia in the United States Supreme Court. And they hired one of the best constitutional lawyers in the country to argue their case for them.

The case arose when an Indian named Corn Tassel was apprehended and tried in a Georgia court for killing another Indian. Corn Tassel was found guilty and sentenced to be hanged. The Cherokees—in the case *Cherokee Nation* vs. *Georgia*—appealed to the Supreme Court on the grounds that Georgia lacked jurisdiction over the tribe. John Marshall, the Chief Justice of the United States, declared that the Cherokees were not an independent nation as understood under the Constitution but rather a "dependent domestic nation." In other words, that Indian tribes were dependent upon the federal government, not the states.

But Georgia paid no heed to Marshall. Just a few days before the decision was handed down, Corn Tassel was executed. Still the Cherokees resisted. In another case the Indians again appealed to the Supreme Court. Again it involved a Georgia law. This particular law forbade white men from residing among Indians without obtaining a license from state authorities. Two missionaries named Worcester and Butler disobeyed the law and were arrested and imprisoned. In the case *Worcester* vs. *Georgia*, John Marshall declared the Georgia law unconstitutional, stating that Georgia had no constitutional right to extend her authority over the Cherokee Nation. Andrew Jackson supposedly said when he heard the decision, "Well, John Marshall has made his decision. Now let him enforce it." This may sound like Jackson, but there is no real evidence he ever said it.

But whatever Jackson said, he was determined to initiate the policy of removal, even as the Congress prepared to act. His Secretary of War wrote to several army generals stationed in the Southwest in 1829 and ordered them to arrange Indian agreement to the government's policy of removal. "A crisis in our Indian affairs has arrived," he wrote, because of the action by Georgia. This action was certain to be imitated by other Southern states that wanted to get rid of Indians. The President, he continued, was convinced that the only way they could escape destruction "is *for them to emigrate.*" But Jackson wished to avoid trouble, the Secretary said. Therefore the generals must convince "the chiefs and influential men" of the Southern tribes with reason and logic of the necessity of removal. If the chiefs could be brought around, "the rest would implicitly follow." Avoid a general council, he continued, because then those who oppose the idea could raise objections and influence others. Instead, if the chiefs could be spoken to individually and privately they might be persuaded by forceful argument. The generals should say something to the effect that the "President views the Indians as the children of the Government. He sees what is best for them; and that a perseverence in their refusal to fly the dangers that surround them, must result in their misery, and final destruction."

Two themes were hammered at by the Jackson administration: The policy of removal adopted by the President was necessary to preserve Indian life and culture; and refusal by the Indians to remove themselves would result in the destruction of the race. That a government of free men could threaten the destruction of a race of people to accomplish its will is a sad commentary on democracy in the Age of Jackson.

Whether the Indians agreed to their own removal no longer mattered. The white men had determined they must go, and go they would, *now.* Responding to Jackson's request, Congress passed the Indian Removal Act in 1830. According to this act, Indian lands within the existing twenty-four states were to be exchanged for new lands west of the Mississippi River. Nothing was said about forcing the Indians to go if they resisted relocation. On the surface the legislation appeared decent and humane. Then, a few years later, in 1834, Congress enacted the

Indian Intercourse Act, setting up the Indian Territory which later became the state of Oklahoma. The Indians were expected to live in this Territory, where they were promised perpetual protection from the white man.

Thus, the solution of the Indian problem seemed easily resolved in the cooperative act of Congress and the administration, both responding to the nation's desire to expand westward without the presence of the Indian impediment. There were some objections. Petitions came from college students and some religious groups such as Quakers, Methodists, and Congregationalists, begging the government to protect the Indians in their claims to their own land as well as to allow them the exercise of their own laws and customs. To do otherwise, said these petitioners, would be unjust and oppressive. But this token concern for the Indians nowhere matched the concern for the slaves which was mounting at precisely the same moment in time. The verdict of Americans in the Jacksonian age was that Indians belonged out west on the plains, where they could be ignored and forgotten.

So under Jackson, under the great democratic leader of the American people, the tragic and horrible removal of the Indians began. Whatever the intentions of those responsible for the policy, the actual removal was a frightful injustice which brought sickness, starvation, and death to thousands of human beings.

Some Indians readily complied with the dictates of the government. They ceded their lands in the East, packed their belongings, and headed west into the treeless, waterless, arid plains. Andrew Jackson himself signed over ninety treaties with various tribes—Northern as well as Southern—accepting their eastern lands in exchange for western lands in the Indian Territory.

Not all tribes were so obliging. The Alabama Creek Indians had to be forcibly removed, many of them in chains. The Chocktaws were booted out of Mississippi in the dead of a bitter winter with little provision for their needs. Sometimes Indians were tricked into signing away their lands and possessions, tricked through drink or empty promises. Several times suspicion and distrust and the impatience of the white man triggered Indian wars. For example, when the hungry Sac and Fox Indians in Illinois returned to their ancestral lands to plant grain and escape starvation, the white settlers in the region suspected an attack and proceeded to slaughter them. This was the famous Black Hawk War which Abraham Lincoln participated in. An even more serious conflict occurred in 1835 when the Seminole Indians in Florida, led by a young and able chieftain named Osceola, refused to comply with the treaty they had signed and emigrate. Troops were dispatched to Florida by the President. But the Seminoles, adept at guerrilla warfare, stubbornly resisted, and so a long, ugly war dragged on for years in the Everglades. Even after Osceola was captured under a flag of truce, the Indians continued to fight. But it was hopeless. Although it cost the government over fifteen million dollars, the Seminoles were eventually subdued, their lands taken from them, and most, but not all, of the tribe driven westward.

But a special horror awaited the Cherokees in Georgia. They refused to budge and President Jackson had to threaten them. "You cannot . . . flourish in the midst of a civilized community," he told them. "You have but one remedy. . . . Remove to the west." Using every legal weapon available to them they delayed the removal for several years, but finally in 1838 they were forcibly expelled from their lands. Georgia militiamen were sent into their country. These militiamen were not disposed to treat the Indians kindly, and quickly demonstrated that they meant business. Prison stockades were erected "for gathering in and holding the Indians preparatory to removal." From these forts soldiers with rifles and bayonets went out in search of Indians, flushing them out of house and cabin and bringing them to the stockades as prisoners. Indian families at dinner, wrote one observer, "were startled by the sudden gleam of bayonets in the doorway and rose up to be driven with blows and oaths along the weary miles of trail which led to the stockade. Men were seized in their fields, women were taken from their wheels and children from their play."

Frequently, the captured Indians would turn for one last look at their homes as they reached the top of a hill or ridge only to see them in flames, set afire by the lawless rabble who followed the soldiers and scavenged for loot. These outlaws stole the cattle and other livestock; they robbed graves in their desire for silver pendants and other valuables. One Georgia volunteer who later served in the Confederate army said: "I fought through the Civil War and have seen men shot to pieces and slaughtered by thousands, but the Cherokee removal was the cruelest I ever saw."

Within a single week the efficient Georgia militiamen had rounded up over seventeen thousand Cherokees. These bewildered Indians, homeless, destitute, and hungry, could hardly understand what had

Savagery, greed and utter contempt for human life are nowhere better illustrated than in the story of the Indians' removal from their

ancestral lands. The *Trail of Tears* shows the proud and mighty Cherokees on their long trek into the alien territory of the West.

happened to them. They were herded into a concentration camp. Many sickened and died. In June the first contingent of about a thousand Indians was taken to steamboats and sent down the Tennessee River on the initial leg of the westward trip, a journey the Cherokees came to call "The Trail of Tears." Then they were boxed like animals into cars drawn by two railroad locomotives. Again there were many deaths because of the oppressive heat and the cramped conditions in the railroad cars. The Cherokees walked the last leg of "The Trail of Tears" until they reached their final destination beyond the western border of Arkansas. In all it was an eight-hundred-mile journey.

A handful of Indians hidden away in the uppermost reaches of the mountains was impossible to get at, and because of this tactical problem an incident occurred which produced in Cherokee annals one of its great heroes. According to the best eyewitness accounts, a Cherokee woman was attacked by two soldiers and in self-defense she killed both with a hatchet. An Indian named Tsali took the weapon from the woman and hid it under his shirt so that she would not be charged with the "crime." The American general in charge of the troops served notice on the mountain Cherokees, of whom Tsali was a member, that they must produce someone who could be punished for the homicides. The Cherokees were all for rejecting the demand and taking their chances of escaping capture in their cloud-hidden heights. But Tsali said he was prepared to offer his life for his people, and a white trader and friend of the tribe named William Thomas advised the Indians to accept Tsali's offer—but with conditions. The general was then informed that Tsali would be surrendered to the Americans for punishment in return for permission for the rest of the Cherokees to remain in the mountains unmolested. Since the general was anxious to avoid a difficult campaign in the mountains, he agreed to recommend the proposal to his superiors in Washington. Meanwhile Tsali was brought in by a contingent of Cherokees and handed over to the Americans. In one of the most ghastly displays of American justice, the contingent of Cherokees who had accompanied Tsali were required to execute him. Tsali, his brother, and his eldest son were lined up before a firing squad and shot.

For years the white trader, William Thomas, attended the prolonged negotiations to win over both the state and the United States to the proposal of allowing this tiny band of Cherokees to remain undisturbed in their mountain hideaway. Since so few Indians were involved, since the land they occupied was unattractive and inaccessible, the state and federal governments finally gave their consent and Tsali's sacrifice was rewarded. The descendants of those Cherokee stalwarts still live in those mountains today.

The remainder of the Cherokee Nation was not so fortunate. It has been estimated that some four thousand of them died on "The Trail of Tears." Along the way the Cherokees were cheated and robbed by agents, speculators, contractors, lawyers, and anyone wielding local police power. Food provided by the governments disappeared or arrived in short supply. "Oh! the misery and wretchedness that presents itself to our view in going among these people," wrote one man. "Sir, I have witnessed entire families prostrated with sickness—not one able to give help to the other; and these poor people were made the instruments of enriching a few unprincipled and wicked contractors." By the middle of June 1838, the general in charge of the Georgia militiamen reported that no Cherokees remained on Georgia soil except as prisoners in the stockade. It was a very efficient operation, the practical annihilation of a once great people.

All told some sixty thousand Indians were removed beyond the Mississippi, and of that number perhaps fifteen thousand Indian men, women, and children died in transit. It is one of the most disgraceful episodes in American history. Protests from reformers and hundreds of church groups fluttered into Congress denouncing removal. But once the red men were transported across the Mississippi, it was presumed by many men of goodwill that the Indians and their cultures were at last safe. In his last message to Congress Andrew Jackson stated that he thought he had finally settled the Indian problem to the satisfaction of all, that he had saved the race from extinction. "This unhappy race," Jackson said, "are now placed in a situation where we may well hope that they will share in the blessings of civilization and be saved from that degradation and destruction to which they were rapidly hastening while they remained in the States. . . . Our own citizens . . . will rejoice that the remnant of that ill-fated race has been at length placed beyond the reach of injury or oppression, and that the paternal care of the General Government will hereafter watch over them and protect them."

A democratic government freely elected by the people had solved the Indian problem to its own satisfaction. The paternal care of the federal government that Jackson spoke about never occurred. When the American people were ready to move again, across and beyond the Mississippi, the Indians were forced once more to get out of the way.

There was resistance and bloodshed until the prostrate red men could fight no more. Herded into reservations in some of the most desolate sections of the United States, the Indians were practically forgotten, since they no longer had the will nor the strength to protest their fate. Miraculously, many of the tribes survived (just barely), and their cultures too.

And so, in a terrible contradiction, a young republic just starting to emerge as a powerful democratic nation resolved one of its problems by the near extinction of an entire race of people, who, they thought, stood in their way. Yet at the time, many politicians in Congress and in the White House believed they had placed the Indians in a position of safety by settling them across the Mississippi, beyond what Jackson called "the reach of injury or oppression." They thought what they did was their only possible course of action. And maybe, despite everything that happened, maybe it was.

BOOK III
THE GROWTH
OF PRESIDENTIAL POWER

(overleaf) When Jackson tangled with members of Congress during the early 1830s, he restructured the government's balance of power. Here Jackson takes his cane to the many-headed "Hydra of Corruption," the Bank of the United States. In the center, Van Buren explains his distaste for dissention. The individual heads of the Hydra represent state branches of the Bank; the largest head—wearing a top hat—pictures its president, Nick Biddle.

8

The President Vetoes

PERHAPS THE SINGLE most important political event of Jackson's entire administration was the Bank War. Jackson's "War"—and that is the best word to describe his actions—against the Bank of the United States had a staggering impact on the course of American history.

The War reshaped the nation's political future. In fact, in terms of party history, it overshadowed all other events during the middle period of the nineteenth century—roughly the years from 1816 to 1850. It brought about the creation of a new political party, the Whig party. It fashioned the character of the Democratic party with respect to leadership, organizational discipline, and popular following for over a generation. It exalted such things as party loyalty to the point where most issues in the immediate future would be determined in Congress strictly by party vote. And it demonstrated that the President could be a politician of the great mass of American voters as well as head of the party.

Most important, the War altered the fundamental structure of government. The conflict between the supporters and opponents of the Bank, fought both in Washington and across the country, resulted in a vast expansion of presidential power. The fight that ensued between the President and the Congress profoundly changed the relationship between the executive and legislative branches. The operation of government as originally conceived by the Founding Fathers, with its delicate system of checks and balances and its dependence on the supremacy of Congress in originating laws, was altered to such an extent that Henry Clay called it a "revolution . . . tending towards a total change of the . . . character of the Government."

And the War had an economic impact, too. It indirectly produced an enormous expansion of credit and paper money which propelled the nation into an era of significant industrial growth and development. The creation of this capital advanced the full implementation of the industrial revolution.

The Second Bank of the United States, frequently referred to as the BUS, had been created by Congress immediately after the War of 1812. Its capital stock—which was different from its deposits—was assigned at thirty-five million dollars, one-fifth of which was purchased by the United States government and four-fifths by the public, making it a quasi-public institution—partly owned by the government and partly by private individuals. According to its twenty-year charter, the BUS was permitted to expand from its main headquarters on Chestnut Street in Philadelphia and establish branch banks in the leading cities of the country. When full-grown it was like a vast octopus, with its head in Philadelphia and its tentacles reaching to Boston, New York City, Charleston, Cincinnati, Pittsburgh, New Orleans, Savannah, Washington, St. Louis, Natchez, Portland, Buffalo, Nashville, and Baltimore—in all a total of twenty-six branches. Calling it an octopus is not to imply anything sinister; this is just an easy way to describe its far-flung influence and power by the time Jackson became President.

The BUS was run by a board of directors, five appointed by the President of the United States and twenty elected by the stockholders. In actual practice, however, the affairs of the Bank were managed by its president, who was elected by the stockholders.

The Bank not only accepted savings from private depositors, but it also served as the depository for all government monies. In other words, the United States government handed over its funds to the BUS for its care and use. That made the BUS an economic powerhouse. Because it had so much money and so much power, it was the financial center of the United States.

Furthermore, the authority of the Bank to issue bank notes (paper money or IOUs) which could be redeemed in specie (gold and silver) automatically increased the supply of currency in the country. When more money was needed all the Bank had to do was issue more notes. Thus the BUS could expand and contract credit at will. This control of currency and credit supply helped American business because when business needed to expand, money or credit were available as loans from the Bank. Of course, if the Bank wanted to be nasty and refuse loans it could cripple business and cause a recession. In this way—through the instruments of credit and money supply—the BUS centralized and controlled the financial operations of the entire country. It had enormous power for good or evil.

The funds of the federal government which the Bank held on deposit did not simply sit in the Bank's vaults; they were invested. Millions of dollars put to work to make millions more. And these millions were shared by those people at home and abroad who were wealthy enough to own the Bank's stock. Of course the government was a stockholder, too. But four-fifths of the stock was held by private individuals who were well-off for the most part. So to some people it seemed unfair that money taken by the government from *all* the people in the form of taxes was invested by the BUS to make additional money for the wealthy few.

But the government did enjoy certain real and immediate advantages from its arrangement with the BUS. The Bank helped in the collection of taxes. It transferred government funds from one section of the country to another without charge. It also served as a depository for government funds. Despite these advantages, its ability to control the entire fiscal structure of the country seriously disturbed some Americans.

Andrew Jackson was one. He did not like the staggering power available to the Bank through its control of credit and currency. He did not like its ability to act with or without government approval, with or without public support. Like any corporation, the Bank's principal concern was the welfare of its stockholders, not of the public at large. Worse, said Jackson, this financial clout could be employed "to control the Government and change its character." It could be used to influence the political process—by "buying" elections for example—to get what it wanted.

The president of the BUS at this time was Nicholas Biddle. Here was a man who had everything: brains, looks, money, family, taste, and tremendous financial savvy. He came from a well-to-do Philadelphia

125

family, graduated Princeton at the age of fifteen as valedictorian (he could have graduated a year earlier but the trustees of Princeton thought that too young), toured Europe, and served as temporary secretary to James Monroe, who was then the American minister to Great Britain. Upon returning to the United States, Biddle learned law, won election to the Pennsylvania legislature, married an heiress, and was finally appointed to the board of directors of the BUS by President James Monroe. The brightest, most articulate, best-informed member of the board, Biddle was elevated to the presidency of the Bank in 1823.

But Biddle had his faults. He was arrogant. There were also questions about his integrity. Not that he slipped his hand into the till on occasion to augment his income. Rather, some things he initiated violated the terms of the charter. For example, he was not above lending the Bank's money to the Bank's "friends" and refusing loans to those he considered hostile. He showed favoritism to privileged Congressmen, several of whom, including Daniel Webster, received retainers from the Bank.

In his first annual message to Congress, in 1829, Jackson took notice of the BUS. He did it in two short paragraphs. But those paragraphs eventually touched off a War that shook the nation and profoundly affected the processes of government. In the message Jackson said the Bank had "failed in the great end of establishing a uniform and sound currency." He also said he doubted its constitutionality and expedience. But Congressmen hearing these comments could hardly believe Jackson was serious. The Bank a failure at establishing a sound currency? That was absurd. Whatever its sins or faults, the BUS had indeed stabilized and strengthened the currency. Jackson was simply exaggerating.

Yet it was soon clear that the President wanted changes in the Bank's operations. Since the charter was due for renewal in 1836 he invited Congress to begin thinking of reform. He was not out to kill the Bank. Not now, at least.

But Jackson's dislike of the Bank went deeper than he told Congress. As a young man he had gotten involved in a land speculation scheme and accepted some IOUs which turned out to be worthless. Only through luck and hard work did he finally extricate himself from financial disaster. But forevermore Jackson hated IOUs, speculation, paper money, and banks themselves. "I do not dislike your Bank any more than all banks," he later told Biddle quite bluntly. And the reason banks were so high on his hate list was that they speculated in land and paper money, and frequently issued paper in excess of their gold and silver reserves. And where bank speculation ran unchecked, bank failures were extremely common, taking with them the savings of innocent people and wiping them out.

Another thing: Jackson did not believe in credit. Every man should pay his debts just as he himself had done in his youth, when he had nearly collapsed into bankruptcy. Consequently he objected to the paper-issuing, credit-producing aspects of banking. If people paid what they owed in hard money, said Jackson, the country would be better off. Of course it was impossible to get rid of all banks. They were a necessary evil. But Jackson did feel something should be done about the largest of them—the BUS—particularly since it had been created by the federal government. As President, he now had his chance.

Curiously, Biddle wasn't disturbed by Jackson's message to Congress. He told a friend he was convinced the President was essentially friendly to the BUS! After all, he had had a recent conversation with Jackson in which he told the President that he thought he could have enough of the government's money put aside to pay off the national debt by 1833, something Jackson devoutly wished. And not only pay it by 1833 but pay it on January 8, the anniversary of the Battle of New Orleans. It would be a kind of gift to the President to help celebrate the great event.

The conversation had taken place in the White House. Jackson, looking grave, had gestured his guest to sit near the fireplace. Biddle tried to be pleasant and gracious. Elegantly dressed in the latest fashion, he exuded a sense of social and financial power that came very naturally to a member of the privileged class.

"I feel very sensibly the services rendered by the Bank at the last payment of the national debt," said Jackson to Biddle at one point, "and shall take an opportunity of declaring it publicly in my message to Congress."

"We shall all be proud of any kind mention in the message," Biddle replied, "for we should feel like soldiers after an action commended by their General."

"Sir," said the sly Jackson, "it would be only an act of justice to mention it."

Actually the President had no intention of commending the Bank in his annual message to Congress. Quite the contrary. Still, when the message was published, Biddle chose to interpret it as basically

127

friendly. Had the President really meant to make trouble, he thought, he certainly would have devoted more than two short paragraphs to the question.

If Biddle failed to understand Jackson's intention, many people around the country got it—and liked what they got. One New York Congressman wrote: "I have twice read Andrew's message & think it a very good one, for the best of all reasons, because in all important points his Dox agrees with my Dox, which you know is the only way of determining what is orthodox & what heterodox—I shall vote against rechartering the great bank. It is capable of raising too high a pressure for the safety of those who may come within the sphere of its action."

The Bank was too powerful, he was saying. Too dangerous. And any number of people around the country agreed with this Congressman. But they had other objections as well. They felt the Bank was a monopoly with special privileges granted to it by Congress, by which the rich who owned its stock got richer and everybody else paid the bill. Such privileges ran contrary to the spirit of this democratic age, violating the generally accepted notion of the times that everyone should have an equal opportunity to get ahead.

One man summarized other complaints which he heard around the White House. He listed the Bank's "corrupting influence" because of its enormous wealth, particularly since it had Congressmen on its payroll; "its patronage greater than that of the Government"—and the Jacksonians were very sensitive about patronage because they understood its importance to the functioning of a democracy; and, he concluded, "its power to embarrass the operations of the Government— & to influence elections."

Influence elections! Here now was one of the things that really rankled. Here perhaps was the true reason for the Bank War. During the presidential election of 1828 there had been reports that the Bank had used its money against Jackson to assist the reelection of John Quincy Adams and other National Republicans. For example, it was asserted that money had been spent in Kentucky to buy votes among roughnecks and river bums for Adams, and that the branch bank of the BUS in Louisville had contributed $250 to the National Republican party. T.P. Moore, the Democratic party's chief organizer in Ohio, informed Jackson that "Mr. Clay presses the United States branch Bank." That last remark may have been ambiguous, but it was enough to quicken Jackson's already aroused suspicions.

These were trifling incidents, although irritating to Democrats. But

128

when Isaac Hill, the Jacksonian newspaperman and party organizer in New Hampshire, publicly alleged partisan political actions by the Portsmouth branch of the BUS, he fired the shot that touched off the Bank War—or so Webster, Clay, John Quincy Adams, and many other contemporaries later contended.

Here's what happened. According to the Democrats in New Hampshire, Jeremiah Mason, president of the Portsmouth branch of the BUS and a close friend of Daniel Webster, had been discriminatory in awarding loans, refusing the applications of the friends of General Jackson. In addition the branch interfered in the election of Democrats through its financial contributions to the campaigns of National Republicans. In sum, as Hill curtly informed Biddle himself, the "friends of General Jackson have had but too much reason to complain of the branch bank at Portsmouth." They demand "that this institution . . . may not continue to be an engine of political oppression." Mason lent money to his own brother-in-law in Boston, said Hill, but "our" merchants who needed only "two or three thousand dollars" were refused.

As repeated to Jackson and reported in the Democratic press, the lending practices of the Portsmouth branch (which probably reflected the general policy of the BUS, they said) constituted an attack "on the plain people of the North" while the "vested interests" of the upper classes were pampered and subsidized. It was a conspiracy, snapped the Jacksonian newspapers, of wealth against the common good, a "contest between the Bank and the People."

Rather cleverly, the Democrats transformed a complaint about the Bank's political discrimination against their party members into a struggle between the interests of the rich and powerful on the one hand and the interests of the vast numbers of ordinary folk on the other. Partisan politics had spawned a democratic crusade.

Most unwisely, Biddle just ignored Hill's letter of complaint. But when the accusations were repeated by Levi Woodbury, the Democratic Senator from New Hampshire, and Samuel D. Ingham, Jackson's new Secretary of the Treasury, Biddle could not ignore them. Nevertheless, his written replies to Woodbury and Ingham were unbelievably inept and can only be described as demonstrations of bad temper. He categorically denied any interference by the Bank in the recent election and attributed the "personal rancor" against Mason to his vigor in enforcing the payment of debts.

To satisfy himself that his conclusions were correct, Biddle took a trip to Portsmouth to investigate the charges. Not surprisingly, his preconceived opinions were amply supported by the people he interrogated. The entire affair, he concluded, was a "paltry intrigue got up by a combination of small bankrupts & smaller Demagogues." All of which he subsequently reported to Ingham, adding gratuitously that it was none of the Secretary's business what the political opinions and actions of the Bank's officers were!

Ingham showed the letter to Jackson. The President read it slowly, studying the tone of the letter. When he finished reading it he returned it to Ingham and after a long pause instructed his Treasury Secretary to inform Biddle that the President of the United States "reserves his constitutional powers . . . to redress all grievances complained of by the people of the interference by the Branches with the local elections of the states, and all their interference with party politicks, in every section of the country."

According to most contemporaries, the Portsmouth incident began the Bank War. Even if one challenges this oversimple explanation of a major historical event, the Portsmouth affair certainly initiated the rhetoric and tone—thanks to Hill, Woodbury, and many other politicians, as well as an efficient Democratic press—which converted partisan political complaints against the Bank into a democratic crusade for social, economic, and political justice. Out of their pique over the Bank's failure to support their election, Democrats found an issue by which they could champion the cause of the people against the rich, or, as they put it, "the Democracy against the Aristocracy." Of course they identified their opponents, the National Republicans, as the party of the "aristocracy."

But what resulted from the crusade was never contemplated by the promoters of the Bank War. What resulted was a number of significant—indeed "revolutionary"—changes in the structure and process of government.

The influence of party politics on the life of the BUS became absolutely clear when Biddle decided to ask Congress for a renewal of the Bank's charter in 1832, four years before its current charter expired. He was opting for a trial of strength between the President and the Bank, even though he was warned that in such a trial "the Bank will go down—For Gen J's popularity is of *a sort* not to slaken at present."

Then why did Biddle permit such an action, when it might cause his

Bank's destruction? Quite simply, many National Republicans wanted him to request an early renewal of the charter because they could then make an election issue of it; this, they felt, could aid their reelection in 1832. Or, since Jackson was also seeking reelection, he might see it to his advantage not to allow the matter to become an issue and thus permit the Bank to have its recharter. Obviously Biddle could ill afford to disregard the wishes of the National Republicans, for, "The friends of the Bank in Congress," he was told, "expect the application to be made."

So Biddle asked for recharter. And immediately his action was interpreted by the Democrats as a challenge to the reelection of Andrew Jackson. "Now as I understand the application at the present time," wrote Roger B. Taney, Jackson's Attorney General, "it means in plain English this—the Bank says to the President, your next election is at hand—if you charter us, well—if not—beware of your power." Biddle was deliberately baiting the President, said Taney. He dared Jackson to "do his d——dest."

The application for recharter instantly roused Jackson's fighting instincts. When an assistant spoke to him about being forced under the circumstances to grant recharter, Jackson started raging. "I will prove to them that I never flinch," he stormed, "that they were mistaken when they expect to act upon me by such circumstances." As far as the President was concerned, Biddle's latest action only confirmed his belief that the Bank interfered with the political process and was therefore dangerous to the government and the people. An institution so monstrous had to be destroyed. Not changed, not reformed. Executed!

In his letters the President began to refer to the Bank as a monster, a "hydra-headed" monster, equipped with horns, hooves, and tail, and so dangerous that it impaired "the morals of our people," corrupted "our statesmen," threatened "our liberty," subverted "the electoral process," and sought "to destroy our republican institutions." The Democratic press repeated Jackson's litany and explained to the people how Biddle's request for recharter actually disguised an attack upon the President and the great American electorate. "The Jackson cause," they trumpeted, "is the cause of democracy and the people, against a corrupt and abandoned aristocracy." And why is the President opposed, they asked rhetorically. Because "he supports the interests of the WHOLE PEOPLE—because he will not uphold corrupt monopolies— because he will not become suppliant to the Aristocracy of the land! *This*

131

Thomas Hart Benton was Jackson's most important floor manager in Congress. As one friendly politician observed of their Bank war, "They were the chief destroyers of the *monster*."

is why he is opposed. And who are his opposers? Do they class with the farmers and mechanics? No. Do they class with the useful—the laboring men of the country? No. They are the rich—the powerful—the men who grind the faces of the poor, and rob them of their hard earnings. Men who live on their *twenty per cent extortions* from the poorer classes. *These* are the opposers of Andrew Jackson.''

"Let the cry be heard across the land," stormed the Washington *Globe*, the principal Democratic newspaper. "Down with bribery—down with corruption—down with the Bank." That also meant "down with the National Republicans," the friends of the Bank.

So the issue was joined. Biddle demanded recharter now. Jackson insisted the Bank must go. In January 1832, a bill for recharter was introduced into Congress and the two parties—the National Republicans and Democrats—lined up for battle. In the Senate, Henry Clay, the presidential candidate of the National Republican party, and his colleague Daniel Webster took the lead in guiding the bill's safe passage through Congress, while Jackson's friend and supporter Thomas Hart Benton, Senator from Missouri, commanded the opposition. Biddle, of course, was on the scene using "his" money and influence to aid the Bank's cause. He ordered petitions sent to Congress from every state in the Union. He bought advertising space in newspapers to argue the Bank's position. He reminded influential politicians of past favors.

And Biddle's efforts paid off. On June 11, 1832, after a long debate, the bill for recharter passed the Senate by a vote of 28 to 20; a month later, on July 3, by a vote of 107 to 85 it rode through the House of Representatives. Biddle was overjoyed. "I congratulate our friends most cordially upon this most satisfactory result," he wrote. "Now for the President."

Jackson was waiting. Debilitated by the hot, sticky July weather, the President looked like a ghost when the Bank bill came to his desk for signing. Some feared he was close to death. He was sixty-five years old and recently had had another "bleeding of the lungs," probably caused by an abscess from his old wounds. He had barely enough strength to get out of bed. Van Buren came to see him one day and was startled by the President's appearance. The old man lay on a couch, gasping for breath. As Van Buren walked into the room Jackson glanced up, his face brightened, and he grasped his friend's hand. "The bank, Mr. Van Buren, is trying to kill me," he said in a whisper. Then, pressing Van Buren's hand very tightly, he added, *"but I will kill it."*

133

His message vetoing the Bank bill was ready. It had been prepared by several members of his Kitchen Cabinet, most notably Amos Kendall, Roger B. Taney, Andrew Jackson Donelson, who was the President's nephew and personal secretary, Levi Woodbury, and, of course, Jackson himself. And what they produced was a remarkable state paper of transcendent historic significance. Indeed, it was the most important veto message ever written. It changed and amplified the fundamental power of the President.

The Bank veto was sent to Congress on July 10, 1832. It hit like a thunderclap. Jackson cited not only constitutional, but social, political, and economic reasons against the recharter. He said the Bank of the United States enjoyed exclusive privileges that gave it a monopoly of foreign and domestic exchange. Government must never grant exclusive privileges to any institution or individual, he continued, for that necessarily creates inequities and in the United States there must be equality for all. Only a relatively few people own stock in the BUS, yet they divide profits from investment of government funds which are collected from all the people. Worse, some eight million dollars' worth of shares of this stock are held by foreigners, said Jackson. "By this act [passed by Congress] the American Republic proposes virtually to make them a present of some millions of dollars." Over and over in the veto message, like the intense nationalist he was, Jackson reiterated his concern over this foreign influence within the Bank—and through the BUS, the entire country.

In writing the veto the way he did, Jackson accomplished something that was quite unprecedented. Previous Presidents had used the veto a total of nine times! In forty years under the Constitution only nine bills had been killed by a President. And only three of these nine dealt with important legislation. In every instance the President vetoing a particular bill had claimed it violated the Constitution. It was generally believed that a question of a bill's constitutionality was the *only* reason to apply the veto. Jackson disagreed. In his veto he now declared that a President could kill a bill for any reason—political, social, economic, or constitutional—when he felt it harmed the nation. If he thought a measure detrimental to the people's welfare, Jackson insisted the President had a right and a duty to veto that measure.

The implications of Jackson's interpretation of the veto power were enormous. The President was now taking on powers that had always belonged to Congress. This was immediately recognized by men like

134

Clay and Webster. For in effect what Jackson said to the Congress in the Bank-bill veto was this: Before passing any law, you had better be sure I am not opposed to it, because if I am, I have the power to kill it.

Thus, according to Jackson's view, Congress must carefully consider the President's wishes on all legislation *before* enacting it, or risk a veto. This interpretation of presidential prerogatives essentially changed the relationship between the legislative and executive branches of government. For, from the beginning of the nation under the Constitution, the legislative branch of the government—the Congress—had been considered preeminent. In the minds of most, it was Congress that embodied and secured representative government—not the President. Now Jackson seemed to be disputing that. Of course Congress can override a presidential veto, but that requires a two-thirds vote from both houses. Overriding is almost impossible to obtain because of party loyalty; it usually happens only when there are lopsided majorities of the party opposed to the President in both houses. As a result, few presidential vetoes have been overturned since Jackson's time. In effect, then, Jackson was claiming that the power of the President was the equivalent of two-thirds of both houses of Congress! His interpretation of the veto would alter the basic equality between the branches of government as written into the Constitution by the Founding Fathers. Instead of a 50-50 relationship between the chief executive and Congress, it would become a 67-33 relationship in the President's favor.

Continuing his veto message, Jackson next declared that the Bank in his opinion was unconstitutional. That was a shocker. For Supreme Court Justice John Marshall had declared the Bank constitutional in 1819 in the case *McCulloch* vs. *Maryland*. He had decreed that the implied-powers clause of the Constitution authorized Congressional action in creating the BUS.

"To this conclusion," said Jackson in his veto, "I cannot assent." Both houses of Congress as well as the executive must decide for themselves what is or is not constitutional before taking any action, whether that action consists of voting for a bill by Congress or signing it by the President. "It is as much the duty of the House of Representatives, of the Senate, and of the President," Jackson continued, "to decide upon the constitutionality of any bill or resolution which may be presented to them for passage or approval as it is of the supreme judges when it may be brought before them for judicial decision."

National Republicans wondered what Jackson was up to now. Was he attempting to make himself and the Congress coequal with the courts in determining the constitutionality of Congressional legislation? If that was true, he was undertaking still another fundamental alteration in the structure of government.

Although Jackson was challenging the Court's exclusive right to determine constitutionality, he was speaking before, not after, the fact. After the fact the Court decides; before the fact, he was saying, both the President and the Congress have a duty to determine in their own minds the constitutionality of specific legislation and to act accordingly. Jackson was contending that just because the Court declares a bill constitutional does not mean Congress *must* vote for such a bill when one is introduced or that the President *must* sign it if, in their good judgment, they honestly believe the bill unconstitutional. And, on the Bank question, Jackson did not agree with the Court's earlier position. Since the matter was subject to legislative and executive action, he simply claimed the right to think and act as an equal and independent member of the government.

If this doctrine was not electrifying enough to jolt some members of Congress right out of their seats, the final paragraph in the message certainly was. And it did! "It is to be regretted," said Jackson, "that the rich and powerful too often bend the acts of government to their selfish purposes. Distinctions in society will always exist under every just government. Equality of talents, of education, or of wealth can not be produced by human institutions. In the full enjoyment of the gifts of Heaven and the fruits of superior industry, economy, and virtue, every man is equally entitled to protection by law; but when the laws undertake to add to these natural and just advantages artificial distinctions, to grant titles, gratuities, and exclusive privileges, to make the rich richer and the potent more powerful, the humble members of society—the farmers, mechanics, and laborers—who have neither the time nor the means of securing like favors to themselves, have a right to complain of the injustice of their Government."

This was a call to war. It was political propaganda of the highest order, guaranteed to stir men to action. Jackson had converted partisan complaint against the Bank into a struggle between the rich and poor. As champion of the common man—what he called the farmer, mechanic, and laborer—the President was prepared to do battle with the institution that most represented the privileged classes in America. There is almost a touch of demagoguery to the message, in that it can be interpreted in its final paragraph as an invitation to class conflict. But what magnificent propaganda it was! What red-hot controversy!

The message was effective. It caught the spirit of the times and expressed it in forceful language. It recognized that there were differences in society and always would be, but it declared that the government must never interpose to help one class over another and thereby aggravate these differences. When it does interfere, by such actions as creating the Bank, it creates "artificial" distinctions. This generates inequality, which produces injustice. Despite all the differences that existed in society, Americans of the Jacksonian period believed in human equality in the abstract, which they felt could be realized in the concrete as equal opportunity. Perhaps that, after all, is the essence of American democracy, even today.

Jackson ended his veto message by declaring his belief that there were no necessary evils in government. "Its evils exist only in its abuses," he said. "If it would confine itself to equal protection, and, as Heaven does its rains, shower its favors alike on the high and the low, it would be an unqualified blessing. In the act before me there seems to be a wide and unnecessary departure from these just principles."

Friends of the Bank were aghast at the tone and language of Jackson's message, let alone its principles. Nicholas Biddle likened it to "the fury of a chained panther biting the bars of his cage." It was, he said, "a manifesto of anarchy, such as Marat or Robespierre might have issued to the mobs" during the French Revolution.

The battle now moved back to Congress. Clay, whose American System dictated the need for sound currency and credit through the efforts of a strong bank, and Webster, who as the principal spokesman for American capitalism advocated a central bank, undertook the difficult next step of trying to convince Congress to override Jackson's veto.

Both Houses of Congress were jammed with spectators when the debates began. In the hall of Representatives visitors had to listen very carefully because the acoustics were so poor. Sounds skidded around the walls before ascending into the great dome ceiling that rose sixty feet above the floor. Otherwise the chamber was a model of governmental splendor, with a Brussels carpet covering the floor, crimson curtains over the windows and also beneath the low gallery, and a vast quantity of brass spittoons located around the room within firing distance of every Representative. Huge brass candlesticks adorned the Speaker's desk, over which hung an immense canopy of crimson silk with a

137

superimposed gilt eagle. Columns of Potomac marble topped by white Corinthian capitals supported the semicircular hall and provided a majestic setting for the dramatic debates which were about to begin.

The Senate appointments were even more luxurious. Because there were fewer members than in the House, the atmosphere had an intimacy that encouraged powerful exchanges among the strong-willed, opinionated, and colorful personalities who made up the Senate. When Webster rose to denounce Jackson's veto message it was a foregone conclusion that he would deliver a mighty blast. The gallery hushed when he began to speak.

"According to the doctrines put forth by the President," intoned the glowering Webster, "although Congress may have passed a law, and although the Supreme Court may have pronounced it constitutional, yet it is, nevertheless, no law at all, if he, in his good pleasure, sees fit to deny it effect; in other words, to repeal and annul it." More than that, Webster continued, Jackson "claims for the President, not the power of approval, but the primary power, the power of originating laws."

Not exactly. Rather Jackson claimed the right to be a partner in the power of originating laws, a power he argued was lawfully his under the Constitution by virtue of his veto authority. But even this was a departure from the past. Up to this time, the power of originating laws had always been presumed to be lodged exclusively with the Congress. So Webster rejected Jackson's claim. "We have arrived at a new epoch," he warned. "We are entering on experiments with the government and the Constitution, hitherto untried, and of fearful and appalling aspect."

Henry Clay agreed with Webster. And when he asked to speak there was even greater excitement among visitors in the galleries. For Clay was a gut fighter, a verbal brawler whose slashing attacks on his victims delighted his audience because they were always so deliciously nasty and personal. He called Jackson's action a "perversion of the veto power." This power, he said, was "not expected . . . to be used in ordinary cases. It was designed for instances of precipitate legislation, in unguarded moments." It was to be used rarely, if at all, something all previous Presidents had understood. Jackson's interpretation, on the other hand, was "hardly reconcilable with the genius of representative government."

The Democrats hooted at Clay's criticism. Thomas Hart Benton, Jackson's staunch ally in the Senate and a man so opposed to paper money that he was called "Old Bullion," defended the President's message and chided the opposition for its lack of respect for Jackson. He rebuked them particularly for their abusive language. But Clay, in reply, laughed at Benton's present solicitude for the General. He remembered back to 1813, he said, when Benton, Benton's brother Jesse, and Jackson had a disagreement that ended in a gunfight in Nashville. At least, taunted Clay in a sneering tone that brought laughter from the galleries, "I never had any personal rencontre with the President. I never complained of the President beating a brother of mine after he was prostrated and lying apparently lifeless." Nor, he continued, had he ever said that if Jackson were elected President, Congressmen would have to protect themselves by carrying knives and pistols.

"That's an atrocious calumny," cried Benton, springing to his feet.

"What," retorted Clay, "can you look me in the face, sir, and say that you never used that language?"

"I look," said Benton, "and repeat that it is an atrocious calumny, and I will pin it on him who repeats it here."

Clay flushed with rage. "Then I declare before the Senate that you said to me the very words."

"False! False! False!" screamed Benton.

Other Senators jumped to their feet, fearful the two men would attack one another. Ladies in the galleries let out cries of apprehension while the men roared their excitement at the possibility of a fistfight on the floor.

The chair gaveled for order. After a few anxious moments the dignity of the Senate was restored.

"I apologize to the Senate," said Benton, "for the manner in which I have spoken—but not to the Senator from Kentucky."

Clay responded quickly. "To the Senate I also offer an apology—to the Senator from Missouri, none!"

Despite the great burst of oratorical power of such Bank men as Webster and Clay, Congress was unable to override Jackson's veto. On July 16, 1832, both houses adjourned. Since there would be a presidential election in the fall, the members were terribly concerned about what the Bank War might mean in political terms. And because of the veto, Jackson had placed the issue squarely before the American people and asked them for a decision. Since Clay had already been nominated for the presidency by the National Republican party and Jackson was the declared favorite of the Democrats, the electorate had a clear alternative. It was either Clay and the Bank—or Jackson and no Bank.

The decision was up to the American people.

9

The Issue Goes to the People

THE PRESIDENTIAL ELECTION of 1832 was one of the most innovative elections in American history. To start with, this was the first (and one of the very few) elections in which the American people were actually invited to decide an important issue. The electorate was frankly told that the life of the Bank of the United States hung on their choice between the two presidential candidates, Jackson and Clay. The election would decide the fate of the BUS. In most presidential elections it is the individual candidate and his party who normally attract the most attention and concern. There may be a platform with promises of legislation to be enacted or reforms to be initiated, but they are not binding and it is rare that an administration fulfills its entire pledged platform. It is even rarer that a significant national question is taken to the people directly with an understanding that however they vote, their decision will be absolute. Probably most voters don't wish to face such an awesome responsibility. They believe such decisions should be left to politicians; after all, that's what they get paid to do. Then if they make a wrong decision, or one that offends a majority of the people, they will be turned out of office.

Politicians understand all this and normally do their utmost to spare the public the burden of decision. The 1832 election was something of an exception.

This election was also significant in that it inaugurated the practice by the major parties of holding national nominating conventions to choose their presidential and vice-presidential candidates. Local conventions and state conventions had become regular practice in many sections of the country in the past few years. But there had never been a national convention. Prior to 1832, presidential candidates had been nominated by caucuses—meetings of Congressional members belonging to the same party, who named their candidate by majority vote—or by state legislatures that usually put forward favorite sons. These techniques were ultimately discarded because they did not seem democratic enough (caucuses) or because they appeared too parochial and local (state nominations). A national convention, comprising delegates from every state in the Union, was expected to provide a more representative device in keeping with a changing, modern society; it would necessarily involve a great many more people from all sections of the country—every state in fact—in the process of choosing presidential candidates. It was another step in the continued democratization of American institutions.

Still another unique feature of the 1832 election was the appearance of the first third party in American history. The Anti-Masonic party began in New York because of a murder in 1826. Suddenly, people became conscious of the existence of a secret society in their midst, the Masonic Order, which, it was alleged, had arranged the abduction and probable murder of a poor stonecutter who had published a book revealing Masonic secrets. Masons were believed to be rich. So the murder was seen as a plot by the "aristocracy" to protect their clandestine organization. The more these agitated New Yorkers inquired about Masonry, the more their suspicions were aroused. They convinced themselves that Masons held all the important positions in politics, law, and business, and that no one could "get ahead" without becoming a member of this secret, undemocratic society.

Soon a political witch-hunt commenced. Anti-Masonic newspapers were founded to fan the fury of the masses. Organizations were formed with the avowed purpose of removing all Masons from political office. During the next few years this furor spread from New York into Pennsylvania, Vermont, and parts of Indiana and Ohio. Some commentators saw the agitation as an ugly aspect of a changing society in

141

which those "on the make" raged against the alleged advantages of privileged classes. Whatever the reason, the movement expanded rapidly, stimulated by the organization and political skills of such men as Thaddeus Stevens, Thurlow Weed, William Seward, John C. Spencer, Samuel A. Foot and Henry Dana Ward. Anti-Masonic parties were organized in several states to screen political candidates and make certain they were free of Masonic taint. When it was discovered that both Jackson and Clay were Masons, the Anti-Masons rejected the candidates of the two major parties and decided to run their own candidate for President.

On September 26, 1831, the Anti-Masons met in Baltimore and held America's first national presidential nominating convention. Thirteen states were represented by 116 delegates at the convention, and they nominated William Wirt of Maryland for President and Amos Ellmaker of Pennsylvania for Vice-President.

But the national convention was not invented by the Anti-Masons. It was something a great many politicians had been talking about for several years. Indeed, back in 1826 Van Buren had suggested a national convention to nominate Jackson in order to strengthen the organization of the emerging Democratic party. Nothing came of the idea at the time because there were fears that a fight over naming the Vice-President might develop, which would seriously injure the fledgling party.

Now in 1832 such fears no longer existed. And because of the continued demand for a more representative, more democratic, method of selecting presidential candidates, the convention system seemed ideal. So it was seized upon by the two major parties.

The National Republicans acted first. They held their convention in Baltimore on December 21, 1831. In all, 155 delegates attended, representing eighteen states, and Henry Clay of Kentucky and John Sergeant of Pennsylvania were chosen to head the ticket. At this convention the delegates voted by roll call—each man rising from his seat when his name was called and declaring the name of his candidate.

A few months later another National Republican convention met in Washington, D.C. to name its candidate. This was a local convention, not a national one. But what made this meeting unique and important was the dramatic appearance of the candidate himself to accept the nomination. Henry Clay was their choice. And suddenly, there he was, standing in their midst, smiling and expressing his pleasure over their action. In a short speech he conveyed "the deep and grateful sense which I entertain for the distinguished proofs which you have . . . given to me of your esteem and confidence.'' If elected, he promised to maintain the people's interest at home and abroad, eradicate corruption, and uphold the Constitution and the laws. And so from this modest beginning would later come the long tradition of acceptance speeches by presidential candidates who would urge the party to fight hard and promise to carry out a program to advance the nation's interests ''at home and abroad.''

Another unusual aspect of this convention in Washington was the decision to write a party platform. Basically, the members adopted Clay's American System at the same time that they condemned what they called ''Jackson's spoils system.'' They also demanded better trade relations with the West Indies.

The Democrats held their convention on May 21, 1832. Some 334 delegates—more than twice the number at the other two conventions—representing every state but Missouri (whose delegates could not reach the convention in time) met in Baltimore. There was no question about the presidential nomination. The incumbent president was their only choice. So instead of nominating him, the delegates simply said they ''concurred'' in the many nominations Jackson had already received from several states.

The real question for the Democrats was the vice-presidential nomination. Jackson wanted Van Buren. But not every Democrat was exactly crazy about the Little Magician, particularly the old friends of John C. Calhoun. Yet what could they do other than desert the party? Jackson had named his choice. So be it. On the second day the delegates duly rubber-stamped it. Jackson and Van Buren became the Democratic ticket.

The convention system, as adopted by the Anti-Masons, National Republicans, and Democrats, succeeded in a number of important objectives. The selection of candidates was conducted in a more open and democratic manner than ever before. More people were involved in the process, and, in time—once the system took hold—they represented every section, state, class, and economic interest and most political views in the nation. The convention eliminated the proliferation of candidates which had frequently happened when selection had been left to individual states. It therefore protected the parties against factionalism and the almost certain defeat at the polls which is its natural consequence. The convention also provided the best technique of forc-

143

ing politicians to close ranks behind the designated ticket even when not everyone is enthusiastic about a particular candidate—as was the case with Van Buren. Party harmony, unity, and loyalty are essential for electoral success, and the convention system, more than anything else, provided this. In an age when the franchise increased rapidly, some process was needed to direct, channel, and guide this vote, lest it be dispersed and weakened over a wide variety of factions and candidates. If the weight of the majority vote is to be felt effectively it must be held together as a majority, not fragmented into a number of minority groups, such as occurred in Europe. The purposes of democracy were therefore well served by the invention of the convention system, just as Van Buren had predicted. It still thrives today, although not everyone is totally happy with it.

In the presidential campaign of 1832 which followed the nominating conventions, the Democrats cleverly argued that the Bank's money was the principal issue, that its financial strength was such that it could always sweep aside popular opinion to get what it wanted. It could bowl over the government too—even influence the election decisively in Clay's favor. This was a genuine fear among Democratic politicians, not a fake issue concocted for popular consumption. "The U.S. Bank is in the field," reported Senator William L. Marcy of the Albany Regency, "and I cannot but fear the effect of 50 or 100 thousand dollars expended in conducting the election in such a city as New York." The fear was repeated in other parts of the country. "The Bank is scattering its thousands here to affect us," reported a New Hampshire man. A Western Democrat declared: "I fear the Bank *influence* more than anything else. I have no doubt that the Bank managers will expend a large sum of money." Said another: "If the Bank, a mere monied corporation, can influence and change the results of our election at pleasure, nothing remains of our boasted freedom except *the skin of the immolated victim.*"

So the contest, as far as the Democrats saw it, was a struggle between unbridled financial power, privilege, and elitist rule in support of Henry Clay on the one hand, and equality, liberty, and popular rule in support of Andrew Jackson on the other. "The Jackson cause," they trumpeted, "is the cause of democracy and the people, against a corrupt and abandoned aristocracy."

One can be very suspicious of such campaign arguments. One can question the motivation behind these exaggerated statements about what

144

the opposition represented. But that's not the historical significance of this election. What was important was the tone and spirit the Democrats generated during this campaign. Their exaggerated boasts and wild claims saturated the atmosphere with cries against privilege, deference, and elitism and in support of popular rule. The people were wise and virtuous in all things, said the Democrats, and their will the only criteria for a free nation. This upsurge of admiration and respect for the people, this vocal affirmation of the merits of a mass electorate, replaced traditional notions of rule by the "few and the wellborn." Like the controversy over "spoils," this election provided the opportunity for politicians to create an ambience of political rhetoric that encouraged the growth of the democratic spirit.

The Democratic party was not alone in this endeavor. The National Republicans made their contribution too, only their bugaboo was not the "monster Bank" but what they called the "corrupt and arbitrary rule" of Andrew Jackson. And his recent veto flouting Congress' decision to recharter the Bank was the latest example, they said. To the National Republicans the election of 1832 was a struggle for representative government against the machinations of a dictator. "THE KING UPON THE THRONE: *The People in the Dust!!!* " read one newspaper headline. Andrew Jackson "has set at utter defiance the will of the people as strongly expressed by their Senators and Representatives . . . he has exercised a power that no Monarch in Europe dared attempt . . . he has, by his frequent exercise of power which should never be ventured upon but in the most extreme cases, proved himself to be the most absolute despote [*sic*] now at the head of any representative government on earth." This nation was created, said the National Republicans, to escape monarchical rule. The Founding Fathers, in their wisdom, provided representative government through the establishment of a Congress elected by the people. And now what's happened? Now what have we got? Now, to subvert republican rule, a President has emerged, elected by the electoral college, who uses the veto to assume power expressly delegated to the Congress. Unless he is hurled from office by the judgment of the people, warned the National Republicans, the nation under executive rule will rapidly collapse into a dictatorship.

The spoils system Jackson had "inaugurated" was another case in point, another example of presidential "despotism." The National Republicans claimed that Jackson had driven men of ability and dedication from office and replaced them with political hacks intent on finan-

145

GRAND FANTASTICAL PARADE, NEW-YORK, DEC 2ª 1833

Humor, absurdity, and downright zaniness—such were political campaigns, as shown in this cartoon, "Grand Fantastical Parade." The flag at the left says: "OUR GENERAL!! May he *soon* meet his *reward* in Heaven for his *everlasting* services on EARTH."

cial gain. In so doing, they said, he was sinking the government into corruption, its integrity irreparably damaged. Only the voters could restore the system to its republican purity and simplicity by directing the removal of Democrats and their replacement with National Republicans, who were devoted to public service and representative Congressional government.

There was still time. "One more opportunity—*perhaps the last*—is yet afforded us," commented a National Republican newspaper in Ohio, "of strangling the monster of despotism before it shall have attained its full growth, and checking the full tide of corruption before it shall have become too strong to be resisted. The power still remains in our hands. Let us so use it as men who are to render an account to our God, to our country, to the world—and all will be well."

Both parties accepted the principle that the great masses of plain people throughout the United States should rule. Whereas, thirty years earlier, Alexander Hamilton had called the people a "beast" and John Adams and other Founding Fathers expressed fears that anarchy was the natural consequence of democracy, in the Age of Jackson these fears evaporated in a celebration of the mass electorate.

One of the important aspects of the 1832 election was the degree to which both parties now attempted to encourage popular participation in the electoral process. They were extraordinarily inventive in persuading people to vote, building on the initial efforts of politicians in the 1828 election. They conducted barbecues, rallies, parades, and the like, recognizing that these techniques tended to bring the people out and get them to vote—and, after all, that was one of the things democracy was supposed to be about. The traditional notion that voting should be confined to the educated or wellborn was forever gone.

Parades became fixtures of American elections and were conducted by all parties, even by men who thought them crude, vulgar, and tasteless displays of the human condition in its worst setting. One of the best such demonstrations in the 1832 election took place in New York City and was described by Michel Chevalier, a Frenchman traveling through the United States at the time. It was a parade stretching a mile long, he wrote. "The Democrats marched in good order, to the glare of torches; the banners were more numerous than I had ever seen them in any religious festival; all were in transparency, on account of the darkness. On some were inscribed the names of the democratic societies or sections: *Democratic young men of the ninth or eleventh ward*; others

147

bore imprecations against the Bank of the United States; *Nick Biddle* and *Old Nick* were figured largely. Then came portraits of General Jackson afoot and on horseback; there was one in the uniform of a general and another in the person of the Tennessee farmer, with the famous hickory cane in his hand. Those of Washington and Jefferson, surrounded with Democratic mottoes, were mingled with emblems in all designs and colors. Among these figures an eagle, not a painting, but a real live eagle, tied by the legs, surrounded by a wreath of leaves, and hoisted upon a pole, after the manner of the Roman standards. The imperial bird was carried by a stout sailor, more pleased than was ever any city magistrate permitted to hold one of the strings of the canopy in a Catholic ceremony. From further than the eye could reach, came marching on the Democrats. I was struck with the resemblance of their air to the train that escorts the viaticum in Mexico or Puebla. The American standard-bearers were as grave as the Mexican Indians who bore the sacred candles. The Democratic procession, also like the Catholic procession, had its halting places; it stopped before the homes of the Jackson men to fill the air with cheers, and halted at the doors of the leaders of the Opposition, to give three, six or nine groans.''

The National Republicans matched the Democrats in organizing parades and rallies. The bigger the better, they said. At one demonstration ten thousand people supposedly attended. "We looked around," wrote one reporter, "and we saw the mariner and the merchant, the storekeeper and the mechanic, the manufacturer and the day laborer—all glowing and gratified at the eloquence of the orators." The rally turned out to be a particularly "glorious one for our cause. It reanimated our friends, added warmth to their patriotism—and has given fresh ardour to their exertions." And at a "great meeting of naturalized Irish citizens" held in Philadelphia and described as a "bumper" crowd, Jackson was repudiated by the overwhelming sentiment of the audience. "Thousands upon thousands were there," reported one man, and "we consider this meeting as a death blow to the administration in this quarter. . . . It is evident that the mass of the people—the bone and sinew of the city and county—the patriotism and purity of the community, are opposed to the re-election of Andrew Jackson."

There was now an exuberance, an "ardour" to the electoral process that generated huge crowds at all party functions. Barbecues were especially attractive. Even when they lost local elections, as the Democrats did in Kentucky, the politicians seemed to think a barbecue was in order. "There seems to be no way of convincing these fellows,"

148

snapped the Louisville *Journal*, a National Republican paper, "that they are fairly beaten. They have one sort of answering for every thing. If we show them that we have elected our Lieutenant Governor by a majority of nearly 30,000, *they reply by swallowing a pig.* If we show them that we have gained great strength in the Senate, and added to our superiority, *they reply by devouring a turkey.* If we show them that we have obtained a majority of two-thirds in the House of Representatives, *they reply by pouring off a pint of whiskey or apple-toddy.* There is no withstanding such arguments. We give it up."

If Democrats were quick to swallow a pig to reply to political argument, the National Republicans showed a remarkable flare for political cartooning as a device to ridicule the opposition. Political cartoons developed into an art during this Jacksonian age. One of the most striking, entitled "Uncle Sam in Danger," showed the good Uncle sitting in a chair, his arm lanced, with blood and gold and silver coins flowing from the wound into a basin held by Amos Kendall. "Dr." Jackson stands over the victim, a scalpel in his hand. "Hold the Bason [*sic*] Amos," says Jackson, "this is merely an Experiment but I take the Responsibility." To one side of the picture Van Buren comments that he cannot give an opinion on the operation, while on the other side stands a citizen who laments: "Twixt the Giniril (since He's taken to Doctring) and the little Dutch Potercary, Uncle Sam stands no more chance than a stump tailed Bull in fly time."

One popular cartoon showed Jackson receiving a crown from Van Buren and a scepter from the devil; another portrayed Jackson, Van Buren, and others attired as burglars, aiming a large battering ram at the Bank's front door; and a third, depicting the spoils system, had a fearsome red devil flying over the country with strings attached to his fingers, feet, and tail, and tied at the other end to spoilsmen who bounced and jumped as the devil jiggled the strings. Presumably Jackson was the devil and the Democrats his puppets.

All of the cartoons and other gimmicks measured the distance politicians had traveled away from serious discussions of important public issues. The tactics marked the level of "debate." A striking pamphlet can influence voters, remarked one commentator, "and so does a well-conducted newspaper; but a hickory pole, a taking cry, a transparency, a burst of sky rockets and Roman candles (alas! that it should be so!) have a potency over a large third of our voters that printed eloquence can not exert."

Perhaps politicians showed keen insight into the public mind by amusing them with hickory poles and Roman candles rather than frightening them with serious talk about the one issue that had been taken directly to them for resolution. It was one thing to talk about democracy, equal opportunity, aristocracy, and privilege, and something else to prove that the Bank had failed to establish a uniform and sound currency or that paper money was a threat to the Republic and that the people by their vote must rid the country of both. Better to cheer Old Hickory—or razz Harry of the West. That way the seriousness of the matter could be concealed and forgotten.

When the hoopla and ballyhoo ended at the polls, Jackson won a thumping victory. He received a total of 688,242 popular votes, or 55% of the total, while Clay took 473,462 votes (37%) and Wirt 101,051 (8%). In the electoral college it was a sweep. Jackson won 219 votes, Clay 49, and Wirt 7. Wirt carried Vermont and Clay took Massachusetts, Rhode Island, Connecticut, Delaware, and Kentucky, and a majority of the Maryland electoral vote. All the rest went to Jackson except South Carolina which, because of the nullification furor, gave her 11 votes to John Floyd of Virginia.

Even though they had been told they were deciding the fate of the Bank, the American people, in casting their ballots, most likely did not vote against the Bank or against Henry Clay as much as they voted *for* Andrew Jackson. The simple truth of the matter is that the masses loved Jackson and had confidence in him and trusted him. He had succeeded in making them feel he was their representative, their leader. And if he directed the dissolution of the Bank then they would follow along, however worried they might be about the financial consequences. "Who but General Jackson would have had the courage to veto the bill rechartering the Bank of the United States," asked one man, "and who but General Jackson could have withstood the overwhelming influence of that corrupt Aristocracy?" Soon there was talk of a third term. "My opinion is," said the defeated William Wirt, "that he may be President for life if he chooses."

Jackson himself saw his election as a mandate from the people to proceed further than his simple refusal to permit recharter of the Bank and to kill it outright, or at the very least cripple it. So the presidential election of 1832 signaled the beginning of the end of the great Bank of the United States. But it also signaled the continued democratization of the electoral process. The masses of American voters were courted and flattered, urged to exercise their ballot in the interest of improved republican government. Many of the politicians who sponsored the electoral nonsense that typified the 1832 campaign may have been quite cynical about the "democracy," the "wisdom" of the people, and other such slogans they bandied around the country. But whether they were cynical or not, whether they believed their democratic mouthings or not, is irrelevant. What is important is that they created—for whatever reason—a climate of respect and regard for the popular will. The sound and tone of "democracy" engulfed the country. The air was saturated with it. And it endured. It became a permanent part of American politics.

This, then, was one of the great contributions of the Jacksonian era.

10

The President Becomes
the Head of the Government

THE ELECTION OF 1832 was filled with the shouts and sounds of a free people raucously engaged in conveying their will to their elected government. But the election actually proved several things. It proved that Andrew Jackson was not only the head of his party, who could dictate the issues the party must support, but also that he was a masterful politician who knew how to lead the great numbers of American people. The election proved the President of the United States could be—and indeed should be—a leader of the masses. The entire electorate was his constituency. He was its representative. Gone forever was the older notion of an aloof chief executive whose responsibility to the people was only vaguely understood.

And much of this had come about because of the Bank War. It provided the occasion by which Jackson during the election campaign could go to the people and ask for their support against the "monster" in order to safeguard their liberties and protect their government. The War started the process whereby the relations between the people and the central government, and among the several branches of government, underwent structural changes. Those changes continued after the election. Indeed, once the election ended and Jackson was assured of four more years in office, he decided to remove the government's deposits from the BUS, and that decision set in motion a chain of events that produced still another vast increase in the power of the chief executive.

Supposedly, Jackson first expressed his decision to remove the deposits to Francis P. Blair, editor of the Washington *Globe.* It was shortly after the election. The two men were sitting in the White House. Blair was complaining to Jackson that despite the electoral victory and the people's "mandate" to do something about the wicked practices of the Bank, Czar Nick Biddle was spending public funds "to frustrate the people's will." The tiny editor sputtered as he spoke. "He is using the money of the government for the purpose of breaking down the government," Blair charged. "If he had not the public money, he could not do it."

Whether Biddle was actually using public money to "break down the government"—whatever that meant—hardly mattered. The President was quite prepared to believe the worst. Thus, as Blair spoke, piling one accusation of impropriety on top of another, Jackson became visibly agitated. The muscles of his jaw tensed. His eyes flashed. Finally he exploded. "He shan't have the public money!" Jackson stormed. "I'll remove the deposits! Blair, talk with our friends about this, and let me know what they think about it."

When Blair returned with the information requested of him a few days later he was surprised to find Jackson calm and quite composed, almost to the point of nonchalance. "Oh," said Jackson, "my mind is made up on *that* matter. Biddle shan't have the public money to break down the public administration with. It's settled. My mind's made up."

That was typical of Jackson. First came the explosion, the tantrums, the wild threats. But once he made up his mind a mood of calm settled over him, sometimes giving people the wrong impression of his attitude. The decision reached, he was now prepared to act. Jackson summoned his cabinet and informed the members of his intentions. Since by law the Secretary of the Treasury, not the President, was authorized to remove the deposits, and since the incumbent Secretary opposed removal, Jackson decided to appoint a new Secretary and "kick" the present one "upstairs" by making him Secretary of State. William Duane, an intense, fidgety, sharp-featured man, was chosen as the new Treasury Secretary because he was known to oppose the Bank and could be expected to do what the President instructed. In a weak moment Duane

153

also agreed to resign his office if he found Jackson's directions impossible to obey.

But once sworn into office, Duane slowly changed his mind about the removal of the deposits. His pride was the chief reason. He did not like the way it was simply presumed that he would do as he was instructed, as though his opinions didn't matter in the least. Finally, since the law clearly placed the responsibility for the public funds in his hands, he decided he was not going to have the responsibility taken from him and was not going to be told—even by the President—what to do. So he went to Jackson.

The President was in his office, sitting at his desk and reading several reports. He greeted his Secretary warmly and the two men sat down together near the window to catch the slight breeze that stirred the hot, humid air. When Duane finished his statement, the President just stared at him, flabbergasted.

"But you said you would retire if we could not finally agree," said the President after recovering from the shock.

"I indiscreetly said so," Duane replied, "but I am now compelled to take this course."

The words angered the old man, as though they had been deliberately chosen to offend him. Still, he did not wish to quarrel with his Secretary and so he tried to reason with him. But Duane would not yield.

"A secretary, sir," said Jackson at one point, "is merely an executive agent, a subordinate, and you may say so in self-defense."

"In this particular case," responded Duane, "congress confers a discretionary power, and requires reasons if I exercise it. Surely this contemplates responsibility on my part."

Duane had a point. The law clearly stated that Duane must report to Congress any decision regarding the deposits. Congress was in recess, and so he felt he should do nothing until Congress reconvened the following December, when he could make his report as the law required.

Jackson seethed. "How often have I told you," he continued, "that congress cannot act until the deposits are removed."

Duane asked for a delay—at least ten weeks.

"Not a day," barked the President, "not an hour."

Now there was only one recourse, and the President quickly took it. Duane was promptly notified in writing that "your further services as Secretary of the Treasury are no longer required." In his place Jackson appointed Roger B. Taney, who had been serving as Attorney General.

This incident may seem trifling. Actually it was extremely important. It was another action which served to strengthen the presidency. It was one more Jacksonian stroke that altered the relations between the executive and the legislature and contributed to the growth of presidential power. To begin with, the purse strings of public funds are held by Congress. This is clearly written in the Constitution. In fact the purse strings are placed in the hands of the House of Representatives, whose members are directly elected by the people. Under the charter of the Bank of the United States, Congress permitted the Secretary of the Treasury to act in its place and remove the government's money if he felt it was necessary. Congress had authorized the Secretary of the Treasury, *not* the President. What is more, the law specifically stated that the Secretary must notify the Congress of his actions. Jackson, in ordering the removal, assumed control of public funds. This action was constitutionally questionable but obviously one which would add to his prerogatives and enhance his powers if he got away with it.

Another reason why this Duane incident is important is Jackson's presumption that he could dismiss at will any member of the cabinet. Since all cabinet posts are created by act of Congress and appointments to them require confirmation by the Senate, there was some question as to whether the President could remove a cabinet officer without receiving prior consent from the Congress. This was particularly true of the Secretary of the Treasury because of his handling of public funds, which fall under the exclusive control of the Congress. Jackson, by his action, settled the question for himself and for all future Presidents. He assumed absolute power to remove cabinet officers without even notifying Congress, much less obtaining its consent. Jackson was asserting exclusive control over the entire executive branch at the same time he was insisting on the right to share some of the powers of the legislative branch.

Here, again, Jackson was breaking with the past, striking off in a new direction. Previous Presidents had resolved difficulties with their cabinet officers by getting them to resign. It was less messy that way, and it also skirted the constitutional question of the President's removal power. But Jackson hit the question head on. His dramatic dismissal of Duane set a precedent. In effect he was defining his authority in such a way as to strengthen presidential prerogatives. And anyone who disagreed with his definition could expect to be summarily bounced out of office.

Duane's dismissal caused quite a storm. There was a barrage of complaints from National Republicans over the President's action. Again, they charged, he was destroying representative government in the United States. "Executive despotism," they called it. They were even more outraged when Jackson appointed Roger B. Taney the new Secretary, and Taney, though not yet confirmed by the Senate, ordered the removal of the government's deposits from the BUS. His order went out in September 1833 and the Congress was not scheduled to reconvene until December 1833. To National Republicans the action appeared to be an outright and illegal assumption of power. Technically, they said, Taney was not the Secretary since he had not been confirmed, but here he was moving public funds in obedience to the President's order.

By the time Congress reconvened, the removal operation was well under way. Actually, Taney did not pull all of the government's money out of the BUS in one fell swoop. His policy was more subtle. He directed that all future money collected by the government in taxes, land sales, tariff revenues, and the like be placed in selected state banks, called "pet banks" by the opposition. For operating expenses the government drew out its remaining funds from the BUS until they were exhausted. Thus, removal was a gradual process and calculated to prevent undue shock to the banking system.

Once back in session, the Senate, under the leadership of Clay and Webster, was spoiling for a fight. An unconfirmed Secretary was directing the dispersal of public funds. What's more, the House of Representatives, which held the purse strings, had the year before voted a resolution declaring the government's deposits safe within the vaults of the BUS and requesting that they be left there. But Jackson had blithely disregarded this resolution and had ordered his Secretary to begin removal. Oh, the clamor and tumult of the Congressional debates once the session got under way. The frustration! the anger! The Senate finally took its fury out on poor Taney. It refused to confirm him as Secretary of the Treasury.

Some Congressmen then argued that since Taney had never been confirmed, he had never been Treasury Secretary and therefore his order for removal lacked legal force. But that argument had no effect on the President and he went right ahead with removal, appointing Levi Woodbury of New Hampshire as the new Secretary of the Treasury and instructing him to continue Taney's policy.

Then came an unexpected shock. Not from Jackson but from Czar Nick. As frustrated and angry as any Senator or Representative, Biddle ached to wreak revenge on his tormentor. "This worthy President," he wrote, "thinks that because he has scalped Indians and imprisoned Judges* he is to have his way with the Bank. He is mistaken." To demonstrate what he meant, Biddle called for a general curtailment of loans throughout his entire banking system. Those seeking loans would be denied; those in debt to the Bank would be called upon to pay what they owed.

Biddle's order was so sudden and its financial effect so devastating that it pitched the country into an economic panic. Which was precisely what Biddle wanted. If he brought enough pressure and agony to the money market there would be such a public outcry that Jackson would be forced to restore the deposits. And maybe the charter, too. Nothing can be accomplished, Biddle wrote, unless there is "distress in the community. Nothing but the evidence of suffering abroad will produce any effect in Congress. . . . Our only safety is in pursuing a steady course of firm restriction—and I have no doubt that such a course will ultimately lead to restoration of the currency and the recharter of the Bank."

Within a few months Biddle reduced loans by more than eighteen million dollars. State banks were directed to pay what they owed the "monster," and pay in hard cash. This squeeze staggered the commercial and manufacturing centers of the country, which needed capital for expansion. "The distress among the merchants is truly appalling," commented one businessman. Dealers and merchants in New York City were reported to be "in very great distress nay even to the verge of General Bankruptcy." "Things are getting worse and worse here," one New Yorker informed Biddle. By the end of January 1834 the pressure was described as "as great as any community can bear." "Bankruptcy to the North is almost general," exclaimed Senator John Tyler from Virginia in February 1834, "and where the present state of things will end it is impossible to say."

Biddle's arbitrary and disruptive action seemed to prove every accusation Jackson and the Democrats had ever leveled against the BUS. Here was raw, naked power, exercised by one man, who could virtually bring down the financial community throughout the nation without answering to anyone except his money-hungry board of directors. Of course friends of the Bank responded by accusing Jackson

---

*During the Battle of New Orleans Jackson arrested the federal district judge for issuing a writ of habeas corpus releasing a man the General believed dangerous and had had imprisoned.

of abuse of power, to which the Democrats replied that Jackson had at least been elected to his office by the people of the United States, that he exercised legitimate authority granted under the Constitution, and that his actions proceeded from his concern for the welfare of the people, not the mercenary interests of the wealthy few. Again and again, Democrats interpreted the Bank War in terms of Jackson as champion of the people versus Biddle the spokesman of the money power.

During the winter and spring of 1833-34, Jackson received repeated pleas from businessmen to give in to Biddle so that he would end the curtailment. They assured the President that he had demonstrated his great popularity with the masses and had won a stupendous electoral victory. "But give Biddle his charter," they begged, "or he will ruin us." One delegation told the President that they were close to bankruptcy, that they were insolvent.

"Insolvent do you say?" snorted Jackson. "What do you come to me for, then? Go to Nicholas Biddle. We have no money here, gentlemen. Biddle has all the money. He has millions of specie in his vaults, at this moment, lying idle, and yet you come to *me* to save you from breaking. I tell you, gentlemen, it's all politics."

Indeed! And no one knew that better than Andrew Jackson. Yet it was the kind of politics that ultimately served the democracy, for the Bank War revealed the inherent dangers and impropriety of government participation in financial operations that enrich or benefit one class of citizens over all others. Jackson saw, too, how the Bank had been used to serve political ends, such as the 1832 campaign of Henry Clay, and he repeatedly warned how threatening the consequences of such involvement could be to the liberty of the nation.

As a matter of fact the Bank War led immediately into a realignment of political parties. Under the combined pressure of Jackson's removal policy and Biddle's financial squeeze, a new political combination slowly emerged in the winter of 1833-34. All those who hated and feared Jackson and the aggressiveness of his presidency—National Republicans, Bank men, Southern nullifiers, states' righters, friends of Calhoun, Democrats who could not accept removal of the deposits—joined together to form a new political party. They called it the "Whig" party, which is the classic name used to designate opposition to concentrated political power in the hands of the chief executive. The name was first employed in the newspapers and received national attention when Henry Clay used it in a speech attacking Jackson which he delivered in the Senate on April 14, 1834.

The old National Republicans, who had originally coalesced in support of a vigorous federal government to advance the economic and intellectual well-being of the nation, now found their ranks swelled by men who disagreed with their political philosophy but who joined them for a variety of reasons: Jackson's use of presidential power, or his Bank policy, or the way he handled the nullification controversy, or the spoils system—all the things he had done to curtail Congressional authority and thereby, it seemed, representative government. Many were former Democrats—especially Southern Democrats—who believed he had indeed misused his office. Others were Northern businessmen who thought Jackson's reckless assault on the Bank would financially damage the nation. Soon the Whig newspapers were attacking Jackson as "King Andrew the First" and describing him as a despot plotting to extinguish the liberties of the nation. Cartoons showed Jackson garbed as an emperor, with a crown on his head and a scepter in his hand. Under his feet was the tattered Constitution. The Whigs contended they were locked in a deadly struggle with a tyrant who confused his own will with the people's. Their duty was to alert the people to their danger and pull the tyrant down.

Despite the formation of the Whig party, despite their attacks, despite the anguished cries of bankrupt merchants because of the panic, Jackson would not change the thrust and direction of his presidency nor budge from his resolve to kill the Bank. "I have it *chained*," he raged, "*the monster must perish.*" To give in to Biddle now, he argued, would be to surrender the freedom of the nation to a money changer who did not represent them or care for their interests.

Led by Henry Clay, the Whigs in Congress began a systematic attack on Jackson, accusing him of subverting the republican system of government. They charged him with seeking to transform the country into a dictatorship. "The premonitory symptoms of despotism are upon us," said Clay in one speech before the Senate; "and if Congress do not apply an instantaneous and effective remedy, the fatal collapse will soon come on, and we shall die—ignobly die—base, mean, and abject slaves; the scorn and contempt of mankind; unpitied, unwept, unmourned."

Clay's speech infuriated Jackson. "Oh, if I live to get these robes of office off me," he seethed, "I will bring the rascal to a dear account."

There is a story, undoubtedly apocryphal, that years later Jackson on his deathbed was asked if there was anything he had left undone. "Yes," gasped the dying man, "I didn't shoot Henry Clay and I didn't hang John C. Calhoun."

Jackson was the first President lampooned by his enemies as a monarch, fully ensconced in a throne room and adorned with the robes and symbols of royalty.

BORN TO COMMAND.

OF VETO MEMORY.

HAD I BEEN CONSULTED.

KING ANDREW THE FIRST.

KING ANDREW

THE FIRST,

" *Born to Command.*"

A KING who, possessing as much power as his Gracious Brother *William IV.*, makes a worse use of it.

A KING who has placed himself above the laws, as he has shown by his contempt of our judges.

A KING who would destroy our currency, and substitute *Old Rags* payable by no one knows who, and no one knows where, instead of *good Silver Dollars.*

A KING born to command, as he has shown himself by appointing men to office contrary to the will of the People.

A KING who, while he was feeding his favourites out of the public money, denied a pittance to the *Old Soldiers* who fought and <u>bled</u> for our independence.

A KING whose *Prime Minister* and *Heir Apparent*, was thought unfit for the office of ambassador by the people:

Shall he reign over us,

Or shall the PEOPLE RULE?

The Congressional debates over the removal of the government's deposits from the BUS and Jackson's misuse of presidential power ran on for over three months, the longest single debate in either House or Senate since the government had begun. The seriousness of the matter, the eloquence of the speakers, and the excitement generated by the contest between the President and the Congress drew great crowds of people to Washington.

Washington was still the city of "magnificent distances," which was one of the earliest descriptions of the capital. Government buildings and private homes dotted a sprawling terrain whose streets stretched like spokes of an enormous wheel from the main thoroughfare that connected the White House with the Capitol. Cows pastured undisturbed in the open areas between residences. There was space available for expansion. It was a city planned for the future.

The Senate was the great attraction, for all but one of the great political leaders of the age were clustered there. (Jackson, staying with at least one tradition, remained away from the Senate chamber.) Perched high in his presiding chair was the new Vice-President, Martin Van Buren, looking very composed and debonair. Sprawled in his chair on the floor below him sat Henry Clay, frequently impatient with what he heard in the debate and jumping from his seat to prowl among his colleagues or wander to the Senate table to sample the contents of the snuffbox. Daniel Webster looked grave and worried, his deep-set, luminous eyes peering out under a massive brow. Thomas Hart Benton, the leader of the Senate Democrats, sat among a pile of papers and books ready to demand the floor whenever the attack upon the President descended to low-swinging invective. And then there was John C. Calhoun, his face lined with frustration and disappointment—Jackson's enemy and the outcast of the Democratic party. Because the Senate chamber was small and its acoustics excellent, every snarling, vicious word snapped around the room like the crack of a whip and kept the galleries quiet and unusually attentive.

Both sides claimed to speak for the cause of democratic government, the Whigs in denouncing executive usurpation, the Democrats in assaulting the power of the rich as represented within and without the halls of Congress. Not only Jackson but leaders of both parties suffered savage tongue-lashings. It was something the galleries thoroughly enjoyed. On one occasion during this long debate, Thomas Hart Benton, in a four-day speech, cut up Henry Clay rather badly, and in the process

161

reminded the nation that Jackson had just won an overwhelming popular vote of confidence while Clay had been rejected, put down, defeated. "The senator from Kentucky," he thundered, "calls upon the people to rise, and drive the Goths from the Capitol. Who are those Goths? They are General Jackson and the democratic party—he just elected President over the senator himself, and the party just been made the majority in the House of Representatives—all by the vote of the people. It is their act that has put these Goths in possession of the capitol to the discomfiture of the senator and his friends; and he ought to be quite sure that he felt no resentment at an event so disastrous to his hopes, when he has indulged himself with so much license in vituperating those whom the country has put over him."

But Clay was more than a match for Benton. He returned sarcasm for ridicule, stinging rejoinder for biting accusation. But he never forgot that Jackson was his true target. "Everything [is] falling," he declared in one powerful thrust at the President, "everything [is] going down, down, down." It was a struggle "between the will of one man and that of twelve millions of people. It is a question between power—ruthless, inexorable power—on the one hand, and the strong deep-felt sufferings of a vast community, on the other."

At one point in the debate Clay demanded the attention of Martin Van Buren, the presiding officer. In his most sarcastic voice he "implored" the Magician to go to Jackson and on bended knee "exert his well-known influence" over the President and insist upon the restoration of the deposits. When the speech ended, Clay returned to his seat and smiled at his Whig friends, rather pleased at the digs he had scored at the expense of the Democratic leadership. Everyone turned to Van Buren to catch a reaction but the little man let no meaning slip over his face. Instead he quietly gestured another Senator to take his seat as presiding officer as he hopped down to the floor. Then he walked straight across the chamber toward Clay. There was no mistaking where he was headed and suddenly it occurred to everyone in the room that a fearful brawl was about to take place on the Senate floor between the Vice-President of the United States and the nation's most distinguished Senator.

Seeing Van Buren approach, suspecting the worst, Clay slowly rose from his seat and stared at the approaching figure. Could it be that the Vice-President, that soul of courtesy and amiability, was about to strike him or demand in ugly phrases satisfaction on the dueling grounds? Clay could not imagine what to expect, nor could the spectators who watched in hypnotic fascination. Still Van Buren came on, still headed straight for the Kentucky Senator. Finally he reached Clay's side. The silence in the room now reached thunderous proportions. There was the little man from New York staring up at the tall, gaunt orator from Kentucky. But Van Buren did not rebuke Clay with violent word or action. He bowed. Then, in a mocking voice, he said, "Mr. Senator, allow me to be indebted to you for another pinch of your aromatic Maccoboy." The words snapped the tension and the Senate breathed a sigh of relief as Clay, dumbfounded, waved his hand toward the gold snuffbox he always had on his desk. He was too amazed to utter a word. Van Buren took a pinch of snuff, applied it to each nostril, and then leisurely returned to the Vice-President's chair, winking at Senators as he went. It was a sly, characteristic rejoinder to the Westerner's sarcasm.

The dispute in all its many ramifications had now become a titanic political free-for-all. Democratic leaders organized mass meetings throughout the nation to denounce the "aristocratic" Senate and its master, the "monster" Bank. For their part, Whigs arranged the submission of hundreds of petitions to Congress demanding the renewal of the Bank's charter so that the economic panic could be terminated. One outraged Whig from Cincinnati wrote directly to Jackson. "Damn your old soul, remove them deposites back again, and recharter the bank, or you will certainly be shot in less than two weeks and that by myself!!!"

The "aristocratic" Senate—so named by the Democrats because the Whigs held a slight majority in the upper house—climaxed the furious antics of the past several months by bringing forward a resolution of censure against the President of the United States. So strong was the new Whig coalition and so distressing the economic havoc caused by Biddle's squeeze that on March 28, 1834, under the masterful leadership of Henry Clay, the Senate agreed by a vote of 26 to 20 to officially censure Andrew Jackson for removing the government's deposits from the Bank of the United States without the express authorization of the United States Congress. This, according to Clay, constituted a gross misuse of presidential power.

"It's all politics," Jackson had once said. Now he knew how true his words were. Now he knew how deep a political wound could penetrate, for the censure was a savage blow to his pride. He was crushed by the Senate's action. Always a proud man, a man who guarded his reputation with fierce concern, he was genuinely grieved by the censure.

But not for long. Within a few days the old fighting spirit stirred

163

within him. His blood was up. Although sixty-seven years old and physically quite infirm, he could still summon the will to shout his defiance. With the help of a number of his advisors he began writing a "Protest" message to defend himself before the Senate, but more particularly to defend himself and his actions before the American people.

In the nineteenth century Presidents did not appear in person before Congress. So Jackson's "Protest" had to be read to the Senate, the words droned out by the clerk. And even though the reading lacked dramatic force, the words themselves were so potent—indeed revolutionary—that many Whig Senators, astounded at the appalling doctrines Jackson pronounced in his message, sat staring in utter disbelief.

The President's "Protest" began by accusing the Bank of having grown rotten with financial power, power to control the destiny of individuals and government. "So glaring were the abuses and corruptions of the Bank . . ." he said, "so palpable its design by its money and power to control the Government and change its character, that I deemed it the imperative duty of the Executive authority . . . to check and lessen its ability to do mischief. . . . The [censure] resolution of the Senate . . . presupposes a right in that body to interfere with this exercise of Executive power."

Jackson was a superb politician; he composed his message not simply for the edification of Congress but for the enlightenment and education of the American people. The message was a political document as well as one of the most important and influential state papers ever prepared by a chief executive. Because it was an instrument of propaganda, Jackson felt it important to reiterate his claim that the power of appointing, controlling, and removing those who executed the laws belonged exclusively to the Chief Executive—even though those appointed were confirmed by the Senate and their duties included reporting to the Congress. The Secretary of the Treasury, continued Jackson's "Protest," in a specific reference to William Duane, was subject to the "supervision and control" of the President, and the law establishing the Bank of the United States could not change the relation between the President and his Secretary. Thus, he had had full authority to remove Duane without first obtaining Congressional approval.

Then Jackson dropped the bomb, the thing that had Senators aghast. It separated his administration from everything that had gone before. It

164

changed the whole direction of government. Although it may not sound very important or exciting on first reading because future generations accepted its meaning without question, it actually marked a new beginning in American political history. "The President," declared Jackson, "is the direct representative of the American people." More than that, he is "elected by the people and responsible to them."

Direct representative of the American people! Elected by the people and responsible to them! Those statements convulsed the Whigs. Those doctrines certainly did not accord with the practice or beliefs of previous Presidents. Where was it written in the Constitution and the law, asked the Whigs, that the President was the representative of the people? Where was it written that he was responsible to them? Jackson was obviously repudiating his responsibility to the Congress, where the law and tradition placed it. He was embarked on yet another adventure to strengthen his power by claiming a special relationship to the people—a relationship which he shared with no one else. *Republican government meant leadership by the legislature*, argued the Whigs. *Leadership by the executive meant despotism.*

The entire tone of the "Protest" constituted a dangerous challenge to the traditional theory of legislative government which had, until this moment, been the basis of the American system. As such it could not go unanswered. The biggest Whig guns were trundled out to demolish Jackson's seemingly "monarchical" position and the bombardment began almost immediately. For, without question, they caught all the nuances of the "Protest" in terms of their meaning in relation to the traditional structure of American government.

Daniel Webster was now regarded as the "Great Expounder and Defender of the Constitution"—a title conferred on him by those who considered him "Godlike." It therefore fell to him to open the attack in the Senate and answer Jackson's outrageous contentions.

"Again and again we hear it said," Webster began, "that the President is responsible to the American people! that he is responsible to the bar of public opinion! For whatever he does, he assumes accountability to the American people! . . . And this is thought enough for a limited, restrained, republican government! An undefined, undefinable, ideal responsibility to the public judgment!" Webster paused, his features darkening by the intensity of his feelings. "I ask again, Sir. Is this legal responsibility? Is this the true nature of a government with written laws and limited powers?"

Then Webster confronted Jackson's revolutionary idea that the President was the direct representative of the people, that the executive was in effect the "tribune of the people." Again, Webster denied the principle. "Connected, Sir, with the idea of this airy and unreal responsibility to the public is another sentiment, which of late we hear frequently expressed; and that is, *that the President is the direct representative of the American people.*" At this point Webster was almost shouting. "This is declared in the Protest," he argued. "Now, Sir, this is not the language of the Constitution. The Constitution no where calls him the representative of the American people; still less their direct representative. It could not do so with the least propriety." The obvious proof was the manner of presidential elections.* "He is not chosen directly by the people, but by a body of electors, some of whom are chosen by the people, and some of whom are appointed by State legislatures. Where, then, is the authority for saying that the President is the *direct representative of the People*? . . . I hold this, Sir, to be a mere assumption, and dangerous assumption."

Webster concluded with a vigorous rejection of Jackson's entire theory. "And if he may be allowed to consider himself as the SOLE REPRESENTATIVE OF ALL THE AMERICAN PEOPLE, then I say, Sir, that the government . . . has already a master. I deny the sentiment, therefore, and I protest against the language; neither the sentiment nor the language is to be found in the Constitution of this Country."

The Whigs broke out in wild applause. The hurl and sweep of his language drove them to a near frenzy. With his consummate eloquence, Webster had put it to the President in clear and precise phrases, so that when his speech was printed in the newspapers for the instruction of the American people they would understand: Jackson was deliberately restructuring the government to the advantage of the executive branch, and such restructuring endangered their freedom and liberty, for it was a well-established fact that republican government demanded a strong legislature. Jackson's contentions were the beginning of executive despotism.

Next it was John C. Calhoun's turn to blast away at the President's pretensions. As he rose to speak the Senate and gallery were unusually crowded. Once Jackson's Vice-President, he was now a man without a

---

*See footnote concerning electoral college, page 15.

party. Everyone knew he hated Jackson, but they also knew he was a distinguished political theoretician and whatever he said about the Constitution would have enormous intellectual power.

Calhoun did not fail them. In a lengthy, involved, and strongly argued speech, he assailed the President's claims. Jackson "tells us again and again with the greatest emphasis," Calhoun began, "that he is the immediate representative of the American people. He the immediate representative of the American people! . . . What effrontery! What boldness of assertion! Why, he never received a vote from the American people. He was elected by electors . . . and of course is at least as far removed from the people as the members of this body, who are elected by Legislatures chosen by the people."

"Why all this solicitude on the part of the President to place himself near the people?" Calhoun asked. "The object cannot be mistaken. It is preparatory to further hostilities—to an appeal to the people . . . to enlist them as his allies in the war which he contemplates against this branch of the Government." Calhoun wasn't telling the Senate anything it didn't know. What he did emphasize was the fact that Jackson's appeal to the people masked his attack on the original structure of the government as provided by the Founding Fathers. For, while previous Presidents had understood and appreciated that the seat of government was the Congress, and while they had consequently functioned like prime ministers, as the heads of a coordinate branch of the government—one of the three equal branches—Jackson, on the other hand, now claimed he was the head of the entire government and the spokesman of the American people.

Surely this was pernicious doctrine, concluded Calhoun. It was the destruction of tripartite government. The end of republicanism. The triumph of despotism.

Henry Clay spoke next. Like the others before him Clay denied the President's assertions about his responsibility. "I deny it absolutely," said the Senator. "All are responsible to the law." What Jackson was attempting, he argued, was a "revolutionary" change in government. Everyone who knew anything about the Constitution and the intentions of the men who wrote it could see that. But Clay's speech was not only bitter, it was insulting. The administration, he said, was expiring in agony. If a phrenologist were to examine Jackson's head he would find "the organ of destructiveness prominently developed. Except an enormous fabric of Executive power, that President has built up nothing. . . . He goes for destruction, universal destruction.''

Despite the arguments and eloquence of this triumvirate—Webster, Clay, and Calhoun—Jackson's novel concept found ready acceptance with the electorate, for the people did in fact think of the President as ''their representative''—the man who runs the government. It was an idea whose time had arrived. Perhaps Jackson instinctively knew it, considering his political skills, and knew the people would accept it. Eventually even the Whigs capitulated to it. Said one Senator: ''Until the President developed the faculties of the Executive power, all men thought it inferior to the legislature—he manifestly thinks it superior; and in his hands the monarchical part of the Government (for the Executive is monarchical . . .) has proved far stronger than the representatives of the States.''

In introducing and ultimately finding acceptance of his theory, Jackson altered the essential character of the presidency. As the representative of the American people, the President from this time on became the true head of the government. That meant he would formulate national policy and direct public affairs. Enacting new laws was no longer the sole province of Congress. Instead, the President would present to Congress the needs of the people as he understood them, and ask for the necessary legislation. It was now up to the President to have some vision of the nation's future growth and development (that is if he had any stature as a statesman), formulate the vision into a specific program, and then present the program to Congress for funding and approval.

For all intents and purposes Andrew Jackson was the first modern President. He strengthened the presidency, redefined its role, and profoundly altered its relationship to the people. He used the executive office for purposes of national leadership. Under Jackson the people and their government were brought closer together.

Yet some of the most imaginative politicians of the age did not understand or appreciate what Jackson had done. Some of his closest friends, like Martin Van Buren, had grave doubts about the ''Protest.'' Van Buren feared it might be misunderstood as a denial of the right of Congress to provide for the custody, safekeeping and disposition of the property and public money of the United States. He worried that some might think Jackson had in effect seized this right for the Chief Executive. Van Buren urged him to write a second message and dis-

This 1845 daguerreotype was taken a few months before Jackson's death. Ailments caused by early duels and military wounds bothered him most of his long and active life.

claim any such intention. He felt their political friends might desert them on account of Jackson's policies and actions.

But Jackson was very calm and sure of himself. "Mr. Van Buren," he replied, "*your* friends may be leaving you—but my friends *never* leave *me.*"

By the spring of 1834 the Bank War itself began to move in Jackson's favor. It started when the President, in one more piece of nastiness toward Biddle, ordered the BUS to hand over the funds, books, and accounts (which belonged to the government) relating to pensions for Revolutionary War veterans. In the past the government's money was paid to the veterans by the Bank. Jackson now directed that the payments be handled by the Secretary of War.

Biddle refused. He told the government the money and the accounts were his to handle as he saw fit. But this was very high-handed even if he had been goaded by Jackson. He was saying in effect that he considered himself above government direction, at least above any direction demanded by the President of the United States.

The Democrats lashed poor Biddle over this latest defiance. *He* was the tyrant, they said, not Jackson. Biddle had produced the panic and now he boldly refused a government order to relinquish the pension money. Who exactly did Biddle think he was? Could no government official, no law, command his obedience?

Now even Webster saw the danger. No further argument was needed, he said, to convince the public that the Bank of the United States was a dangerous monopoly and must be dissolved. Still Biddle persisted in his refusal to part with the money. It could not be removed by presidential fiat, he said. It was his to handle as he had always done. And not only did he refuse to give it up, he refused to pay the veterans. Again he thought he could apply financial pressure to get what he wanted. But it was a grave political blunder. All he succeeded in doing was to deepen public resentment toward him and his institution. Without realizing it, and certainly without wishing it, Biddle was helping the President kill his Bank.

Finally, the House of Representatives, where the Democrats held a majority, brought the long War against the BUS to an end. A series of four resolutions was brought in from the Ways and Means Committee, chaired by James Knox Polk of Tennessee, one of Jackson's protégés. The first resolution said the Bank should not be rechartered. The

Democrats lined up solidly behind it and the House overwhelmingly passed it, 134 to 82. The second resolution said the deposits should not be restored to the Bank. Here some Democrats were troubled by the entire removal policy and so the vote was closer, although the measure passed, 118 to 103. The third resolution counseled that the government's money should remain in the state or "pet" banks. It passed by an almost identical vote, 117 to 105. The final resolution called for the selection of a committee to investigate the Bank's affairs and find out the reasons for the panic. By the most lopsided vote of all, the House passed it, 175 to 42.

Jackson glowed. "I have obtained a glorious triumph," he enthused. The vote in the House "has put to death that mammoth of corruption and power, the Bank of the United States."

Criticized by friends and supporters and stung by sharp public reaction to his latest actions, Biddle slowly loosed his financial squeeze. Within a few weeks the panic began to ease. More loans were allowed, more currency made available. It was remarkable, noticed many, how the will of one man could so absolutely control the economy of the nation. Finally, in July 1834, the board of directors of the BUS unanimously instructed Biddle to end the curtailment, and shortly thereafter the panic evaporated. The directors reacted to the temper of public opinion. They knew Biddle was thoroughly despised by the American people. They were now concerned for the life of the Bank.

Without the charter and without the government's funds the Bank slowly died. It was a demeaning death. When Jackson declared that the Bank's notes would no longer be acceptable for payment of taxes owed the government, it was one more nail in the coffin and Biddle began "winding up the Bank's affairs, quietly and certainly." The branch banks became independent state institutions. Finally, after 1836 when the original charter expired, the central bank in Philadelphia ceased to be a national bank and became just another state institution.

The destruction of the Bank of the United States terminated any central control over the nation's banking system, and state banks now enjoyed a vast measure of freedom. So they began issuing millions of dollars of paper money. As a consequence they fueled a mighty spurt of industrial growth and expansion. Since a nation must have capital to become industrialized, one result of the Bank War was extremely important in producing the capital that advanced the creation of America's industrial society.

As for the BUS, its power gone, its commanding position as a financial center was assumed by wealthy Wall Street banks in New York City. And it finally went down in bankruptcy in 1841. Philadelphia ceased being the financial capital of the country. That title now belonged to New York, as Chestnut Street, the site of the BUS, gave way to Wall Street.

In a real sense the Bank War ended a few years later when the Senate, now controlled by Democrats, agreed to "expunge" its 1834 censure of Jackson. For several years the Democrats had tried to expunge but could not overcome Whig opposition. Finally, on January 16, 1837, their ranks swelled by victories in recent elections, they succeeded in passing a resolution to erase the censure from the Senate journal. By a vote of 24 to 19 they directed that black lines be drawn across the words of censure adopted in 1834.

The Whigs were outraged. "It is not in the power of your black lines to touch us," shouted one Whig Senator at his Democratic colleagues. "Remove us. Turn us out. Expel us from the Senate. Would to God you could. Call in the praetorian guard. Take us. Apprehend us. March us off." Webster assured everyone that the action of defacing the Senate journal was unconstitutional, but it remained for Henry Clay to send the fury of Whig resentment and anger ricocheting around the Senate chamber. With almost uncontrolled passion he denounced President Jackson as a tyrant. "He has swept over the Government, during the last eight years, like a tropical tornado," thundered Clay. "Every department exhibits traces of the ravages of the storm. . . . What object of his ambition is unsatisfied? . . . What more does he want? Must we blot, deface, and mutilate, the records of the country, to punish the presumptuousness of expressing an opinion contrary to his own? . . . Black lines! Black lines!" They were black lines surrounding the announcement that liberty was dead in America—constitutional government gone.

When the Whigs had drained themselves of passion and bitterness, Senator Benton was again on his feet to move that the resolution be carried out. As the clerk of the Senate turned to carry out the order most of the Whigs walked out of the chamber to demonstrate their disapproval. Then the galleries set up a commotion. They began hissing the action of the clerk.

Outraged by the hissing, Benton sprang to his feet, his right fist shaking toward the demonstrators. "Bank ruffians! Bank ruffians!" he called out to them. "Seize them, sergeant-at-arms!"

Order was quickly restored and the clerk proceeded to his task. He took the appropriate journal from the shelf, turned to the page of March 28, 1834, when the censure resolution was passed, and carefully drew broad black lines around it. Across its face he wrote: "Expunged by order of the Senate, this 16th day of January, in the year of our Lord, 1837."

It was one of the last legislative actions taken during the administration of Andrew Jackson, a triumph for the Democrats, an action of humiliation for the Whigs.

11

Power and Politics

MARCH 4, 1837, marked Andrew Jackson's last day in office as President of the United States. His eight-year tenure encompassed some of the most important changes in American political history. There would be additional changes in the next several years but to many the brightest, happiest times were those when Old Hickory sat in the White House. They were years of hope and promise. They were the "go ahead" years.

As Jackson prepared to leave the White House and return to his home in Tennessee, he rather enjoyed his reputation as a President who had accomplished a great deal in converting the United States government from an elitest republic into a representative democracy. Not that he had broadened the franchise in any way. But because of his presence, what he symbolized to the nation, and the manner in which the Democratic party capitalized on his popularity, more ordinary citizens were concerned and actually involved in the functioning of their government than ever before. Never a modest man, Jackson appreciated his own achievements as President and he appreciated the depth and intensity of popular feeling toward him. Even Whigs recognized the extraordinary bond between the masses and this fierce, cantankerous old man. The "less informed—the unsophisticated classes of people," wrote one partisan Whig, "believed him honest and patriotic; that he was the friend of the *people*, battling for them against corruption and extravagance and opposed by dishonest politicians. They loved him as their friend.''

Throughout his administration, Andrew Jackson had exercised a leadership new to presidential history. He dared to claim that he was the head of the government. He presumed to set national policy. Furthermore, he insisted that the needs of the American people were best served by strong presidential leadership, meaning the President must be the leader of his party as well as the head of the government.

In augmenting presidential power, Jackson opened a Pandora's box. For presidential power can be used for good or ill, depending on who exercises it. In the course of American history it has been used by some to advance the needs of the people, but it also has been used to subvert constitutional government.

The statesmen of the American Revolution had been very suspicious of a strong Chief Executive. To them, executive power was tantamount to monarchical power, and they had had their fill of monarchical rule. King George III, of late and unlamented memory, was the obvious example of the kind of executive they did not want. When they wrote their Declaration of Independence they listed, point by point, all his abuses of power that had compelled them to rebellion. Consequently, when they came to frame the instrument for their governance—the Articles of Confederation—they abolished the executive office. They believed in legislative government, in their minds the equivalent of representative government. To safeguard the liberty of the people, Congress and only Congress must rule!

The failure of the Articles of Confederation after a six-year trial emphasized the need for a stronger central government. The men who attended the Constitutional Convention in Philadelphia in 1787 understood that one of the weaknesses of the original document was the lack of an executive, so in their new instrument they provided a separate and distinct executive branch. They were still committed to representative government with a strong legislature elected by the people and holding tight the purse strings, but they now created a system of three equal branches—executive, legislative, and judicial—and provided each with the means of checking the others in order to prevent misrule or tyranny.

George Washington was an excellent first President under the Constitution. Not only did he fully implement all the powers provided him by the Constitution, but he infused the office with a style and tone that

175

gave it dignity and importance, something desperately needed to overcome the resentment and suspicion generated by the misdeeds of English sovereigns. Washington jealously guarded his own authority but he was also careful to respect that of the Congress. This worked both ways, for Congress also appreciated the separation of powers and the vigilance necessary for republican government.

Washington's administration constituted the first step in the long development of presidential power. Thomas Jefferson aided the process. A superb politician, he worked his will through his friends on the various committees in both houses of Congress. More important, he decided to buy Louisiana even though there was some question of the constitutionality of such a purchase, a question expressed by himself and members of Congress. Without prior approval by anybody, Jefferson proceeded to make the purchase. And he did it, despite momentary hesitation, because he believed the future greatness and immediate preservation of the Union depended on the acquisition of this territory.

But the first *major* alteration of executive power came with the administration of Andrew Jackson. He redefined the presidency both in its relationship to Congress and to the people. He claimed primacy in government. Of the three equal parts—and they did remain equal despite his innovations—he insisted he was the first among equals, that he was the popular voice, responsible for national policy. No longer a prime minister deferential in all respects to the Congress, he acted as the head of state, the national leader, the formulator of national issues.

This altered interpretation of presidential authority was later strengthened by such notable statesmen as Lincoln, the two Roosevelts, and Woodrow Wilson. Not until World War II did the presidential office undergo yet another and even more fundamental change. It was global war, and the threat of global war that could extinguish life on this planet, that brought a vast expansion of presidential power. By the time the process seemed halted in 1974 by the resignation of Richard Nixon, Presidents had waged undeclared wars, bombed neutral nations, impounded funds appropriated by Congress, and insisted on sweeping claims of executive privilege. What had arrived was what Arthur M. Schlesinger, Jr., has termed an "imperial" presidency.

This concept of limitless executive power, rejected by the nation through the demanded resignation of Richard Nixon, gravely endangered the entire constitutional system of government. Fortunately, the Watergate scandal which ultimately drove Nixon from office terminated (let us hope) this unlawful and loathsome interpretation of presidential power.

But the presidency initiated by Jackson was something else. He represented the concept of a strong president who takes charge of the government, defines the issues, and leads Congress and the nation in achieving the successful resolution of those issues.* It is this kind of presidency that is so essential to the nation's progress and social betterment. Since the adoption of the Constitution it has been the strong President, with a vision of the country's future development, sensitivity to its immediate needs, and the will to eliminate economic and social inequality and injustice, who has secured the legislation that has enhanced the happiness and prosperity of the American people. For it is the President who must decide national priorities and present to Congress the issues requiring legislative attention. To do this he must be a skillful politician as well as a strong-willed executive, for he cannot obtain needed legislation without attracting sufficient votes to win Congressional passage of his program. And his effectiveness in securing votes will depend in large measure on the extent of his party support. In other words the President must be the leader of his party as well as leader of the government if he is to serve the American people successfully.

This type of presidential leadership evolved during the Jacksonian era. To a large extent it happened at this time because Jackson was the kind of man who could exert such leadership and because he was so popular and enjoyed the trust and confidence of the electorate. Also, this leadership developed because Jackson dramatically changed the presidential veto power† and made it a legislative tool. As a consequence, the character of the presidency was also changed.

Furthermore, the kind of leadership Jackson inaugurated was assisted

---

*After Jackson, the notion that the President is in charge of the government became a fact accepted by the American people. A single example will document this.

In 1837 a major depression struck the country. The President, Martin Van Buren, was blamed—after all, he was in charge of the government—and in the next presidential election he was badly defeated. Yet the previous depression, in 1819, had no such effect on the President. James Monroe was not blamed for the catastrophe. Not only was he reelected to office, but it was an overwhelming triumph. He received all electoral votes but one. Obviously something had happened between the presidencies of James Monroe and Martin Van Buren.

†Jackson vetoed twelve times. That's minuscule by today's standards but those twelve constituted more than *all* the vetoes of his six predecessors combined. In addition, Jackson was the first President to use the pocket veto. This is a special veto by which the President may kill legislation by withholding his signature from a bill after Congress has adjourned. If Congress is still in session a bill automatically becomes law ten days after it is passed, with or without the President's signature.

by the revival of a vigorous two-party system and by the intense political activity going on during this period. The recently enfranchised masses were organized into political cadres and marched to the polls to register their preference among the party candidates. In the progress of democracy in America and in the elimination of privilege, the two-party system was a principal contributing agent. It was through this system that voters found the most convenient and effective way of expressing their will.

Also important was the arrival of a new breed of politician who preached the doctrine of popular rule. The politicians of both parties during the Age of Jackson loudly affirmed the merits, virtue, and wisdom of the mass electorate. Traditional notions of deference, privilege, and place, as well as notions about rule by the few, well-educated, or wellborn, dissipated before the democratic blasts about equality of opportunity, the right of every white adult male to vote and hold office, and the indestructibility of a popularly supported government.

President Jackson aided this growth. Not through any direct action of his so much as by the style and tone of his administration. The style bespoke popular rule. It celebrated the masses, even though the nation had a long way to go in providing equal rights for everyone, especially Indians, women, and blacks. Thus, what has been termed "Jacksonian Democracy" is nothing more than the commitment, at long last, to the principal of popular rule. The old fears of the Founding Fathers that democracy could lead to anarchy were finally laid to rest in the shouts and cheers for "the majesty of the people."

One partisan summed it all up when he said that Andrew Jackson gave "an impulse . . . to the democracy of America [which] will always continue to be felt, and impel the government in a more or less popular direction."

The Jacksonian era, therefore, established the fundamental political practices and patterns for the future. It was a new departure in the structure and operation of government. It represented the political beginnings of modern America.

It was also a period in American history when equality of opportunity for all was demanded. The American people wanted to "go ahead," and they savagely resented anything or anyone who had an advantage which could slow them down. So they were on their way. Nothing seemed impossible for them, nothing beyond their grasp. That this age of promise and hope should end in the slaughter that was the Civil War seems a tragic conclusion.

For Andrew Jackson it ended, in a sense, when his chosen successor, Martin Van Buren, followed him as the eighth President of the United States. The day of the inauguration was bright and cloudless. Thousands of people lined Pennsylvania Avenue to witness the beginning of a new administration. But really they had come to salute the departure of the old, for to them there was a deeper and more sentimental attachment to the old than the new.

In the White House, Jackson left his top-floor room for the first time in several weeks, since the onset of his most recent illness. He was just eleven days away from his seventieth birthday and he was a tired and worn-out old man, very infirm and rarely without pain. His face registered his suffering. Though his cheeks were shrunken and he moved stiffly he carried himself with a certain brittle strength. His bearing was always dignified and "presidential," and those glittering eyes notified everyone around that an indomitable, strong-willed, and fiery-tempered curmudgeon still lay coiled behind them.

Jackson slowly made his way out of the White House and seated himself in a carriage beside Van Buren for the drive to the Capitol. For him it was heartening to know that the country trusted him enough to accept Van Buren as his successor. Some politicians said that Van Buren's electoral victory the previous fall was Andrew Jackson's third election as President of the United States. In voting for Van Buren the people once again expressed their faith in Jackson.

As the carriage carrying the two Presidents headed along Pennsylvania Avenue the spectators just stared at the two men. There were no shouts, no applause, no cheers. Just silence. Then, in a profound gesture of respect, they removed their hats. They did it on impulse. They did it without thinking. Thomas Hart Benton was so impressed that he afterward wrote: "For once the rising was eclipsed by the setting sun."

When the two men reached the Capitol a passage was made for them through the immense crowd. Jackson alighted from the carriage and walked steadily through the mass, his tall white head very erect and uncovered. When he reached the top of the portico and could be seen by the vast throng, a "murmur of feeling" generated from the crowd and kept growing in volume until it became a roar. "It was a cry," recorded Benton, "such as power never commanded, nor man in power received. It was affection, gratitude and admiration. . . . I felt an emotion which has never passed through me before." Touched by the demonstration, Jackson turned and bowed to the people below him. It was a simple gesture but it seemed to carry great meaning. The masses responded with a great burst of applause and shouts. Then he took his seat to watch the proceedings.

Van Buren stepped forward to take the oath of office from the new Chief Justice of the United States, Roger B. Taney. This, too, gave Jackson immense satisfaction. He "never forgot his friends," and at the first opportunity he had rewarded Taney for his loyalty, dedication, and ability. On the death of Chief Justice John Marshall he had nominated Taney to fill the vacancy. The number of Whigs in the Senate had long since been diminished, so Taney was duly confirmed by the Democratic majority. It more than made up for Taney's rejection as Secretary of the Treasury a few years before.

After the oath, Van Buren read his inaugural address. At one point he spoke specifically about Jackson. "In receiving from the people," Van Buren said, "the sacred trust twice confided to my illustrious predecessor, and which he has discharged so faithfully and so well, I know that I can not expect to perform the arduous task with equal ability and success. . . . For him, I but express with my own, the wishes of all—that he may yet live long to enjoy the brilliant evening of his well-spent life."

Now it was over for Jackson. Now it was time to retire to the Hermitage. Three days after Van Buren's inauguration the ex-President headed for home, back to Tennessee. He rested along the way and visited many old friends. Because of his many stops it was several weeks before he finally reached Nashville. Wherever he appeared crowds congregated. They seemed to appear from nowhere. As soon as the word passed that General Andrew Jackson was in the vicinity, large numbers of people materialized in an instant. Their genuine affection really stirred the old man. When he spoke to them—and he usually did, because he liked to talk to people—he said he was particularly proud that as President he had "killed the money power" in the country that was oppressing the people. He was also proud that he had put down nullification and saved the Union. But more than all that, he felt he had championed the cause of the ordinary citizen, that he had been a true representative of all the people.

When he finally reached the Hermitage, just outside Nashville, many of his friends were waiting for him. The old men were lined up in front, the boys in the rear. Jackson got out of his carriage, but not without considerable effort. He listened courteously to a welcoming address by a friend. He replied with deeply felt sentiments of his appreciation, after which he shook hands with his old associates. Then one man stepped forward and made a short speech, something to the effect that "the children of his old soldiers and friends welcomed him home, and were ready to serve under his banner." Whenever he called, they would be there.

The words were barely spoken when Jackson began to tremble. His frame shook. Tears streamed down his aged cheeks. The reference to the children was more than he could bear.

"I could have stood all this," he stammered; "but this, it is too much, too much."

The crowd gathered around him and for several minutes there was a general outburst of tears, sentiment, and happy words.

This tough old man was weeping for joy, the joy of satisfaction, of knowing his efforts as soldier and politician had found favor with the people.

Jackson lived on for eight more years. He watched the country suffer through an intense economic depression during most of Van Buren's administration but he was pleased that it held out against establishing another national bank. Economic freedom for the individual, he said, depended on maintaining a divorce between the government and the country's banking operation. In its broadest terms this policy of divorce is called "laissez-faire," a policy the country generally pursued for the remainder of the century.

The depression lasted four or five years and slowed the economic progress of the nation—but did not stop it. By the early 1840s the nation was on the move again.

The depression knocked Van Buren out of the presidency. He was defeated for reelection in 1840 by William Henry Harrison, the Whig candidate who had a reputation as a military hero and an Indian fighter, just like Jackson. But within a month of his inauguration Harrison died of pneumonia and was succeeded by his Vice-President, John Tyler of Virginia, a former Democrat whose economic views strongly resembled Jackson's. In Congress, Henry Clay tried to translate his American System into law, including the establishment of another national bank, but Tyler wielded the mighty veto power and struck down all of Clay's efforts. Some Whigs wanted to impeach the President—they called Tyler "His Accidency"—and they might have tried, if they had had the votes to win conviction.

The decade of the 1840s witnessed a rapid territorial expansion of the United States, which Jackson heartily endorsed. His old friend and protégé, Sam Houston, had gone to Texas and had been instrumental in winning independence for Texas from Mexico. Both Houston and Jackson wanted to bring Texas into the Union but sectional rivalry and the problem of slavery delayed the negotiations. Said Jackson: "Texas [is] the key to our future safety. . . . We cannot bear that Great Britain have a Canedy [*sic*] on our west as she has on the north." Several years passed before the political problems standing in the way of annexation could be resolved. But the Congress finally passed a joint resolution inviting Texas into the Union. As one of his last acts as President, Tyler arranged the formal entry of the new state early in March 1845. Jackson was overjoyed when he heard the news. "All is safe at last," he wrote.

Jackson was also happy to live to see the election of another protégé, James Knox Polk of Tennessee, as America's eleventh President. What added to his pleasure was the fact that Polk had defeated Henry Clay, a candidate for the presidency for the third and last time. Polk was elected on a platform of geographical expansion, for an expansionist surge gripped the country. It was called "Manifest Destiny." The term was coined by John L. O'Sullivan, editor of the *United States Magazine and Democratic Review*, when he wrote that it was the "manifest design of Providence" that Americans would possess "this continent." In other words, God Himself intended this continent for Americans. All others must leave.

Manifest Destiny was an expression of a swelling nationalistic fervor in the country. But there was a danger to it. It could stumble the nation into war. Some Americans demanded the annexation of Oregon. "Fifty-four forty or fight," they cried. But to press for expanding the nation's boundaries to the 54° 40′ line could mean war with England because of her claim to the Oregon territory. Jackson spoke for many fierce nationalists when he said that Polk would maintain the rights of the country, hopefully without resorting to war. "If not," the old man said, "let war come. There will be patriots enough in the land to repel foreign aggression, come whence it may, and to maintain sacredly our just rights and to perpetuate our glorious constitution and liberty, and to preserve our happy Union."

Polk avoided war with England by agreeing to compromise. The Oregon country was sliced in two at the forty-ninth parallel, the northern half becoming part of Canada.

The sharing of the Oregon Territory and the annexation of Texas did not lessen the expansionist fever. California beckoned. But that meant wresting it from Mexico. So be it. In May 1846 the United States declared war against Mexico.

So the Age of Andrew Jackson opened and closed with a bang! The age began with the raucous shouts of an enthusiastic electorate proclaiming the inauguration of Jackson to the presidency—and in the process nearly wrecking the White House. And the age closed with the crackle of gunfire that started the Mexican War and initiated the long, tragic drift into secession and civil war. For the victory against Mexico not only brought in California, but New Mexico, Arizona, Utah— virtually the entire Southwest as it presently exists. And with that, a struggle ensued between the North and the South over whether this enormous territory would be closed or open to slavery. Off and on for a dozen years the struggle raged, only to be resolved in the disaster of the Civil War. The Age of Jackson was over.

Andrew Jackson did not live to witness the hostilities against Mexico. By the spring of 1845 he could no longer keep up the fight. His body throbbed. His head never stopped aching. He coughed incessantly. In addition he began to swell with the dropsy. On June 2, the swelling got so bad that an operation was performed by Dr. Esselman from Nashville. This gave him some relief but it left him prostrate and debilitated.

On Sunday morning, June 8, the doctor visited Jackson at the Hermitage and found him sitting in his armchair. One look and the doctor knew "the hand of death was upon him." Family and friends were summoned. An hour or so later he fainted. Quickly he was moved to his bed, but his family and servants thought he was dead and began wailing their grief.

But the old man hung on. He raised his eyelids. He heard the wails. "My dear children," he whispered, "do not grieve for me; it is true I am going to leave you; I am well aware of my situation; I have suffered much bodily pain." He then took leave of his family, kissing each one and giving each his blessing.

Although the effort was an agony, he spoke again. "My dear children, and friends and servants, I hope and trust to meet you all in heaven, both white and black." There was a pause and he repeated this last phrase, "both white and black," looking at his servants "with the tenderest solicitude." Then he turned and as though in a stupor he just stared at his granddaughter, Rachel.

About noon a neighbor and old comrade in his military and political

183

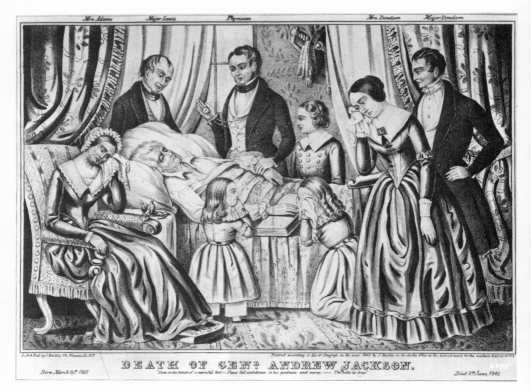

The final scene of Jackson's life in a sentimental rendering. After Old Hickory's death, one of his slaves was asked if he thought the General had gone to heaven. The man thought a moment and replied, "If he wants to go to Heaven who's to stop him?"

wars, Major William B. Lewis, rushed to his side. "Major," said the dying man, "I am glad to see you. You had like to have been too late." Seeing Lewis reminded him to send farewell messages to Thomas Hart Benton, Sam Houston, and other absent friends. Then Jackson lapsed into long silence, his eyes drifting upward into his head. After a few moments, his adopted son took his hand and whispered in his ear, "Father, how do you feel? Do you know me?"

The eyes opened once more. "Know you?" Jackson replied. "Yes, I know you. I would know you all if I could see. Bring me my spectacles."

After the eyeglasses were adjusted to his head, he spoke of his imminent death. Whereupon everyone in the room burst into tears. The servants standing on the porch and looking in through the windows sobbed and wrung their hands.

Jackson spoke again. "What is the matter with my dear children? Have I alarmed you? Oh, do not cry. Be good children, and we will all meet in heaven."

These were his last words. He closed his eyes and lay still. At six o'clock his head fell forward and was caught by Major Lewis. The Major listened for his breathing but heard none. Jackson died quietly.

Major Lewis removed the pillows on which Jackson had been propped. He noticed that the expression of pain so long etched on the General's face had disappeared. The warrior was at rest.

A day later Sam Houston arrived at the Hermitage with his young son. He rushed to the room containing the open coffin. When he saw the corpse he fell on his knees, sobbing. He buried his face on Jackson's breast.

After a moment Houston composed himself and drew the boy to his side. "My son," he said, "try to remember that you have looked upon the face of Andrew Jackson."

Further Reading

ALL HIS LIFE Andrew Jackson was a controversial figure. He still is. Historians have been arguing for more than a hundred years about the man and the period of American history which bears his name. Consequently, many of the things said in this book would cause a few modern historians to howl their disagreement. Some of them even think Jackson and the Jacksonian era an unmitigated disaster for the nation. Edward Pessen, for example, in his *Jacksonian America: Society, Personality, and Politics* (Homewood, Ill., 1969), called the Jacksonian age an age of materialism, of vulgarity, of only *seeming* deference to the common man by a number of *un*common men who really ran things.

At almost every point of the Jackson story different historians take opposite positions, and so this bibliography is constructed to give the reader an opportunity to examine the various contending views.

If Pessen is darkly negative about this era, Arthur M. Schlesinger, Jr., is brightly positive. His *The Age of Jackson* (Boston, 1946), which won a Pulitzer prize in 1946, is still the best overall statement of the era and has not been matched in interpretation or sheer narrative power. To see things from the side of the National Republicans and Whigs (rather than the Democratic side), one should read Glyndon G. Van Deusen, *The Jacksonian Era 1828-1848* (New York, 1959).

Treating Jackson himself there are two admiring biographies: Marquis James, *The Life of Andrew Jackson* (Indianapolis and New York, 1938), which is extremely well written; and my own *Andrew Jackson* (New York, 1966). James Parton, *The Life of Andrew Jackson* (New York, 1860), is long (three volumes), very old, but very good, and ends with an unfavorable interpretation of Jackson.

John C. Calhoun gets the same treatment. A three-volume biography, *John C. Calhoun* (Indianapolis and New York, 1951) by Charles Wiltse, is laudatory; a short biography, *John C. Calhoun: Opportunist* (Gainesville, Fla., 1962) by Gerald Capers, is highly critical. No modern biographies exist of Van Buren or Webster and most of the older ones are limited in value. *The Life of Henry Clay* (Boston, 1937) by Glyndon G. Van Deusen can be read with profit. An excellent biography of Thomas Hart Benton is William N. Chambers' *Old Bullion Benton: Senator From the New West* (Boston, 1956).

The revival of political parties during the Age of Jackson is narrated in Richard McCormick, *The Second American Party System: Party Formation in the Jacksonian Era* (Chapel Hill, N.C., 1966), and Richard Hofstadter, *The Idea of a Party System: The Rise of Legitimate Opposition in the United States, 1780-1840* (Berkeley, Cal., 1969). The Hofstadter book is especially useful and most original.

On the matter of rotation or spoils, James Parton is so critical that he says if all Jackson's other public acts had been perfectly wise and right, "this single feature of his administration would suffice to render it deplorable rather than admirable." Sidney H. Aronson, in *Status and Kinship in the Higher Civil Service: Standards of Selection in the Administrations of John Adams, Thomas Jefferson, and Andrew Jackson* (Cambridge, Mass. 1964), argues that there was little difference between the men chosen for federal office by these three Presidents.

The politicians' handling of the slavery question is probably the most difficult of all to resolve. Ten years ago Richard H. Brown wrote an article, "The Missouri Crisis, Slavery, and the Politics of Jacksonianism," *South Atlantic Quarterly,* LXV (Winter, 1966), pp. 55-72, in which he argued that the question of slavery had a great deal to do with the political alliances concluded during this era. The notion of slavery's significance (rather than the tariff's) in the nullification controversy was developed in William W. Freehling, *Prelude to Civil War: The Nullification Controversy in South Carolina, 1816-1836* (New York, 1965). The argument that national politics of the 1830s were determined by proslavery considerations is forthrightly advanced in Douglas T. Miller, *Then Was the Future: The North in the Age of Jackson, 1815-1850* (New York, 1973).

Abolitionism is traced in a very comprehensive survey by Louis Filler, *The Crusade Against Slavery, 1830-1860* (New York, 1960). A valuable collection of essays on the subject has been edited by Martin Duberman and entitled *The Antislavery Vanguard: New Essays on the Abolitionists* (Princeton, 1965).

Since the turn of the century there has been a growing sympathy among white Americans for the plight of the Indians. This sympathy probably reached its peak in the 1970s. An excellent collection of statements about the Indians has been edited by Francis Paul Prucha: *The Indian in American History* (New York, 1971); this contains a reprint of an important article by Bernard W. Sheehan, "Indian-White Relations in Early America." The best brief survey of Indian history is William T. Hagan, *American Indians* (Chicago, 1961). A sympathetic account of removal is Grant Foreman, *Indian Removal: The Emigration of the Five Civilized Tribes of Indians* (Norman, Okla., 1953), as well as his *The Last Trek of the Indians* (Chicago, 1946). Because of their illustrative material two books are especially valuable: *The American Heritage Book of Indians* (New York, 1961) by William Brandon, and Oliver LaFarge, *A Pictorial History of the American Indian* (New York, 1956). On the Cherokees specifically, see Louis Filler and Allen Guttmann, eds., *The Removal of the Cherokee Nation: Manifest Destiny or National Dishonor* (Boston, 1962). The contribution of the Indians is excellently described by Alvin M. Josephy, Jr., in *The Indian Heritage of America* (New York, 1968).

The Bank War used to be the most hotly disputed issue among Jacksonian historians, but so much was said about it in so concentrated a time span that everyone got pretty sick of it, even though the question of its meaning and importance was never resolved. A brief study is my own *Andrew Jackson and the Bank War* (New York, 1967). Strongly anti-Jackson and pro-Bank is Thomas Govan's biography *Nicholas Biddle* (Chicago, 1959). Also unsympathetic to Jackson and his banking policies is Bray Hammond, *Banks and Politics in America from the Revolution to the Civil War* (Princeton, 1957).

189

Whether democracy really advanced during the Jacksonian era and whether Jackson and his party had anything to do with it are probably the most intensely debated questions now before Jacksonian scholars. This book argues "yes" on both counts. Edward Pessen is probably the one historian who disagrees vehemently, arguing that democracy not only did not advance during this period but actually took a step backward; *Riches, Class, and Power Before the Civil War* (Lexington, Mass., 1973) is his most recent statement on the subject. Although Douglas T. Miller does not deny the rise of democracy in terms of politics during the Jacksonian era, he does insist that aristocracy also grew stronger. His description of the emergence of a new moneyed elite in New York is found in *Jacksonian Aristocracy: Class and Democracy in New York, 1830-1860* (New York, 1967). Lee Benson, *The Concept of Jacksonian Democracy: New York as a Test Case* (Princeton, 1961), argues that both parties—not simply the Democrats as is sometimes claimed—were responsible for the egalitarianism of the period.

The strengthening of presidential power during Jackson's administration is really the subject of my *Andrew Jackson and the Bank War* (New York, 1967); the book's subtitle is *A Study in the Growth of Presidential Power*. Very suggestive is Leonard D. White, *The Jacksonians: A Study in Administrative History 1829-1861* (New York, 1954). Arthur M. Schlesinger, Jr., *The Imperial Presidency* (Boston, 1973), is particularly concerned about the recent rise of presidential power, but he does go back in time and look at the contributions of earlier presidents.

Finally, there are several good general histories of this period, a number of which take an opposite point of view from the one expressed in this book. Furthermore, they discuss social, cultural, and constitutional developments. They include: John R. Howe, *From the Revolution Through the Age of Jackson: Innocence and Empire in the Young Republic* (Englewood Cliffs, N.J., 1973); Douglas T. Miller, *The Birth of Modern America, 1820-1850* (New York, 1970); and Raymond H. Robinson, *The Growing of America: 1789-1848* (Boston, 1973).

Index

Carroll, William (Billy), 47

Catherine the Great, 57

Censure of Jackson, 163; expunging of, 172-73

Chapel Hill College, 47

Character of Americans during the Jacksonian era: "go ahead," 5, 6, 13, 18; materialism, 5, 6, 7, 10, 14, 17; restlessness and mobility, 5, 6, 8, 10; ambition, 5; aggressiveness, 5, 6; work ethic, 7, 8; general appearance, 8

Charles River Bridge Case, 16

Charleston, S.C., 19, 99, 103, 124

Cherokee Indians: culture, 109; controversy with Georgia, 112-13, 115-19; removed, 115-19

Cherokee Nation vs. *Georgia*, 112

Chestnut Street, Philadelphia, 124, 172

Chevalier, Michel, 147

Chicago, 5, 6, 11

Chickasaw Indians, 109

Choctaw Indians, 109, 114

Cincinnati, Ohio, 124, 163

Civil War, 3, 14, 69, 84, 115, 178, 183

Clay, Henry: quoted, 25, 54, 59, 60, 65, 108, 138, 139, 142-43, 159, 162, 167-68, 172; supports John Q. Adams for President, 25, 60, 64-66; early attitude toward Jackson, 25; as party leader, 35, 37, 53, 54, 64; speaking talents, 41, 54, 162; appearance, 53; birth, 54; early career, 54; elected to Congress, 54; elected Speaker of the House, 54; leader of War Hawks, 54; nationalism, 54; ideology, 54-55, 63; critic of Monroe administration, 54; attacks Jackson, 54; proposes American System, 54-55; interpretation of Constitution, 55, 138, 167-68; appointed Secretary of State, 59; criticized, 59; duel with

Randolph, 59-60; and patronage, 60, 61; nickname ("Harry of the West"), 66; opposes Van Buren's appointment as minister, 92; supports compromise tariff, 104; attitude toward Indians, 108, 109-10; supports BUS recharter, 133; presidential candidate, 133, 139, 142, 150, 182; attacks Jackson's interpretation of presidential power, 135, 138, 158, 159, 162, 167-68, 172; response to BUS veto, 137-38; ridicules Benton, 139; defeated (1832) for president, 150; names Whig party, 158; character, 161, 163; challenges Van Buren, 162-63; wins censure of Jackson, 163; and Tyler administration, 181; defeated (1844) for president, 182; incidental mention of, 32, 43, 52, 70, 71, 92, 128, 129, 144

Colt, Samuel, 13

Concord, Mass., 61

Congregationalists, 114

Congress, U.S., 15 note, 23, 70, 103, 111, 113, 123, 139, 176, 182-83; and representative government, 124, 135, 138, 145, 147, 155-56, 159, 165, 175; chambers described, 137-38. *See also* President vs. Congress

—House of Representatives, 43, 59, 64, 94, 170-71

—Senate, 87-88, 163, 164, 172

Constitution, U.S., 3, 4, 15 note, 34, 35, 37, 82, 87, 93, 107, 158, 175; Twelfth Amendment of, 59; and slavery, 93-94, 95, 98; Jefferson's interpretation of, 36, 38, 41; Hamilton's interpretation of, 36, 38; Marshall's interpretation of, 112-13; Jackson's interpretation of, 134-35,

France, 57
Franklin, Benjamin, 24
Freehling, William W., 84
French Revolution, 137

Garrison, William Lloyd, 94-95
Gatsby's Hotel, 34
*Genius of Universal
  Emancipation* (Baltimore), 93
George III, 175
Georgetown, 42, 59
Georgia, 32, 109; and removal of Indians,
  112-13, 115-19
Gibbons vs. *Ogden*, 64
Globe (Washington, D.C.), 71, 133, 153
Goodyear, Charles, 13
Governmental change during the
  Jacksonian era, 3, 18, 66, 70, 74,
  82, 83, 123-24, 130, 134-36,
  152-53, 155, 164-68, 174-76, 177
Great Britain, 9, 15, 24, 43, 54, 57, 63,
  92, 93, 106, 107, 126, 182. *See
  also* British armed forces
Great Lakes, 10
Great Plains, 11
Greene, Nathaniel, 70
Grimké, Angelina, 95
Grimké, Sarah, 95
Grundy, Felix, 43
Gulf of Mexico, 24

Hamilton, Alexander: as Secretary of the
  Treasury, 36; ideology, 36-37, 53,
  147; interpretation of Constitution,
  36, 38
Hamilton, James, Jr., 101-2
Harrison, William Henry, 39, 181
Hayne, Robert Y., 87-88, 103
Hermitage, 27, 29, 111, 180, 185
Hill, Isaac, 71; appearance, 70; attacks
  BUS, 129-30; quoted, 129
Hillsboro, N.C., 46
Houston, Sam, 182, 185

Howe, Elias, 13

Illinois, 4, 10, 11, 93, 114
Illinois and Michigan Canal, 10
Immigrants, 10
Indian Intercourse Act, 113-14
Indian Queen Hotel, 90
Indian Removal Act, 113. *See
  also* Indians
Indian Territory, 111-12, 114
Indiana, 4, 10, 15, 93, 141
Indians, 19, 79; as issue, 17-18, 70, 105;
  Jackson's campaigns against, 23,
  24; frontier attacks by, 24, 25;
  United States policy toward, 105-7;
  early relations with whites, 106-7;
  Enlightenment view of, 107; policy
  of assimilation, 108, 110; removal
  policy developed, 108-9; removed to
  West, 111-12, 114-19; wars,
  114-15; number removed, 119. *See
  also* individual tribes
Industrial changes during the Jacksonian
  era, 9, 10, 11, 14, 43
Industrial Revolution, 9, 124
Inequality during the Jacksonian era, 16,
  17, 106, 108, 178
Ingham, Samuel D., 129, 130
Insane asylums, reforms of, during the
  Jacksonian era, 17
Internal improvements. *See* Public works
International trade, 9
Inventions during the Jacksonian era,
  13-14
Irish, 148

Jack, Gullah, 99
Jackson, Andrew: quoted, 22, 28, 29, 32,
  54, 70, 74, 77, 78, 81, 82, 86, 90,
  92, 102-3, 110, 111, 112, 113, 115,
  119, 120, 125, 126, 127, 131, 133,
  134, 135, 136, 137, 153, 154, 158,
  159, 164, 165, 170, 171, 181, 182;

18, 70, 142ff, 164ff. *See also* Veto

Privilege: economic, 14, 16, 180; political, 14-15, 145, 150, 178; attacks on, 69, 137. *See also* Aristocracy

"Proclamation" message against nullification, 102

"Protest" message against censure, 164-70

Prucha, Francis, 110

Public works, 9, 10-11, 41, 54-55, 63, 64, 108

Quakers, 93, 114

Racism, 84, 106, 107, 108, 110, 113, 120

Railroads, 10-11

Randolph, John, of Roanoke, 59-60

Reaper, mechanical, invented, 13

Reeve, Tapping, 43

Reform movements during the Jacksonian era, 17

Religious reforms of the Jacksonian era, 17

Removal of deposits from BUS, 153-56, 158-59, 162-64, 171

Removal of Indians, 107ff. *See also* Indians

Republican (Baltimore), 70

Revolutionary aspects of the Jacksonian era. *See* Economic, Governmental, Political, and Social changes in the Jacksonian era

Revolver, invented, 13

Richmond Junto, 42

Ritchie, Thomas, 42

Robards, Lewis, 21

Roosevelt, Franklin D., 176

Roosevelt, Theodore, 176

Rotation: importance of, 61, 75, 79, 83; as issue, 69ff, 80; defined, 74, 80; Jackson on, 74, 79, 83. *See also* Patronage

Rubber, vulcanizing, invented, 13

Russia, 57

Sac and Fox Indians, 114

St. Louis, Mo., 124

Salisbury, N.C., 20

Santo Domingo, 99

Savannah, Ga., 124

Schlesinger, Arthur M., Jr., 176

Secession, 61, 63, 64, 84, 87, 101-3, 183

Second Bank of the United States. *See* Bank of the United States

Sectionalism, 17, 85, 87, 104, 182

Seminole Indians: frontier attacks by, 25; defeated by Jackson, 25; removed, 115

Sergeant, John, 142

Seward, William, 142

Sewing machine, invented, 13

Sheehan, Bernard W., 105

Shipping, 9, 63

Slave revolts, 99-100

Slavery, 4, 14, 17, 41, 44, 84, 86, 87, 92, 114; and the Democratic party, 42, 98, 101; defense of, 88, 98-99; as issue, 89, 93-104, 105, 182; and nullification, 101-4

Smith, Gerrit, 95

Smith, Margaret Bayard, 32, 33, 34

Social attitudes during the Jacksonian era, 14-15

Social changes during the Jacksonian era, 3, 5, 6, 11, 13, 14, 17

Society in the Jacksonian era, 6, 7, 17, 141-42

South Carolina, 15 note, 19, 32, 35, 42, 43, 44, 87, 95, 99, 150; and nullification, 101-4

Southwest, 4, 183

Spanish, 19, 25, 54

Specie, 125

Spencer, John C., 142

Spoils system. *See* Patronage

199

Standard of living during the Jacksonian era, 8, 13
Stark, General John, 61
States' rights, 41, 44, 61, 63, 64, 85, 87, 101-4, 158
Statesman (Boston), 70
Stevens, Thaddeus, 142
Story, Joseph, 33, 34
Suffrage, 15, 16, 17, 18, 35-36, 69, 106, 174
Supreme Court, U.S., 16, 31, 33, 64, 112-13, 135
Swartwout, Samuel, 78

Tallushatchee, Battle of, 111
Taney, Roger B., 134; appointed Attorney General, 154-55; removes deposits, 156; appointment rejected, 156, 180; appointed Chief Justice, 180; quoted, 131
Tappan, Arthur and Lewis, 95
Tariff of 1828 ("Tariff of Abominations"), 87, 101, 102
Tariff of 1832, 101-2
Tariff of 1833 (Compromise), 103
Tariffs, 39, 41, 55, 63, 64, 85; opposition by Southerners, 43-44, 65, 101
Taylor, Zachary, 39
Telegraph, invented, 13
Temperance issue during the Jacksonian era, 17
Tennessee, 4, 21, 22, 23, 27, 43, 47, 148, 170, 174, 180, 182
Texas, 182
Textiles, 9
Thomas, William, 118
"Trail of Tears," 118, 119. *See also* Removal
Transportation Revolution, 9, 10, 11, 108
Tsali, 118, 119
Turner, Nat, 99
Tyler, John, 39, 157, 181, 182

Union, 4, 15, 17, 63, 64, 70, 87, 176, 180, 182; as issue, 84-85, 88, 92-93, 98, 101, 103-4; Webster on, 84; Jackson on, 90
United States Magazine and Democratic Review, 182

Van Buren, Martin: quoted, 39, 41, 42, 49, 76, 90, 180; as party leader, 35, 37, 41-42, 46, 48, 49; nicknames ("Little Magician," "Red Fox of Kinderhook"), 38; political skills, 38, 39, 41; birth, 38, 63; and Albany Regency, 38, 75, 80; early career, 39; appearance, 39, 161; character, 39-40, 163; ideology, 41; and patronage, 75-77, 78, 80-81; appointed Secretary of State, 75, 85; rivalry with Calhoun, 85-86; ambition, 85; and nullification, 89-90; appointed minister, 92; rejected by Senate, 92; and Bank War, 133; suggests national convention, 142; vice-presidential nominee, 143, 149; presides over Senate, 161, 162-63; and "Protest" against censure, 168, 170; as President, 177 note, 179; inauguration, 179-80; administration, 181; defeated for reelection, 181
Van Rensselaer, Solomon, 80, 82
Vandalia, Ill., 10
Vesey, Denmark, 99
Veto: early presidential use of, 134; Jackson's use of, 134ff, 177 note; of BUS, 134-35; pocket, 177 note. *See also* President vs. Congress *and* Presidential power
Virginia, 10, 42, 54, 59, 65, 100, 103, 150, 157, 181

Wall Street, 172

Grateful acknowledgment is made for the use of illustrations:

Collection of the Boatmen's National Bank of St. Louis: title page
Faneuil Hall, Boston: 67
Harper's Weekly: 96-97
Library of Congress: 26, 62, 146, 169, 184
The Metropolitan Museum of Art; gift of I.N. Phelps Stokes,
Edward S. Hawes, Alice Mary Hawes, Marion Augusta Hawes, 1937:   58
The New-York Historical Society: 30, 121, 160
The New York Public Library, Picture Collection and Prints Division: 1, 12,
40, 72-73, 81, 91, 132
United States State Department: 56
Woolaroc Museum, Bartlesville, Oklahoma: 116-117
Yale University Art Gallery, gift of John Hill Morgan: 45

About the Author

As Professor of History at the University of Illinois, Robert V. Remini has twice been named Outstanding Teacher of the Year. His scholarship on the Jacksonian period appears in several of his books, including *Martin Van Buren and the Making of the Democratic Party, The Election of Andrew Jackson, Andrew Jackson* (a biography), *Andrew Jackson and the Bank War,* and *The Age of Jackson* (documents). He is consultant to "The Papers of Andrew Jackson," the official project which will publish all of Jackson's important papers and correspondence.

Born in New York City, Mr. Remini earned his M.A. and Ph.D. degrees at Columbia University. He served on the editorial board of the *Journal of American History,* published by the Organization of American Historians. He now lives in Wilmette, Illinois, with his wife and three children.

Format by Joyce Hopkins
Set in Linotron Times Roman
Composed by National Service Corporation
Printed by The Murray Printing Company
Bound by The Haddon Craftsmen, Inc.
HARPER & ROW, PUBLISHERS, INCORPORATED